LETTER TO A NEW PRESIDENT

ALSO BY SENATOR ROBERT C. BYRD

ROBERT C. BYRD: Child of the Appalachian Coalfields

LOSING AMERICA: Confronting a Reckless and Arrogant Presidency

LETTER
TO A NEW
PRESIDENT

—

COMMONSENSE LESSONS
FOR OUR
NEXT LEADER

—

SENATOR ROBERT C. BYRD
with STEVE KETTMANN

THOMAS DUNNE BOOKS
ST. MARTIN'S PRESS ❦ NEW YORK

THOMAS DUNNE BOOKS.
An imprint of St. Martin's Press.

www.thomasdunnebooks.com
www.stmartins.com

Book design by Jonathan Bennett

Library of Congress Cataloging-in-Publication Data

Byrd, Robert C.
    Letter to a new president : commonsense lessons for our next leader / Robert C. Byrd, with Steve Kettmann.—1st ed.
        p.   cm.
    Includes bibliographical references and index.
    ISBN-13: 978-0-312-38302-2 (alk. paper)
    ISBN-10: 0-312-38302-9 (alk. paper)
  1. Presidents—United States.   2. Political leadership—United States.
3. United States—Politics and government.   I. Kettmann, Steve.   II. Title.
    JK516.B97   2008
    352.230973—dc22

                               2008012469

First Edition: July 2008

10 9 8 7 6 5 4 3 2 1

TO MY DEAR WIFE ERMA

CONTENTS

DEAR NEW PRESIDENT *1*

1. BRING BACK THE FIRESIDE CHAT *53*

2. TEACH THE PEOPLE ABOUT THE CONSTITUTION *65*

3. NO LIFE STANDS OUTSIDE OF HISTORY *75*

4. A BIG LIE IS STILL A LIE: TELL THE TRUTH *87*

5. BUILD YOUR PRESIDENCY AROUND ACCOUNTABILITY *97*

6. LET THE PRESS DO ITS JOB, EVEN WHEN THAT MIGHT STING . . *109*

7. WE CAN DO BETTER THAN PHOTO-OP DIPLOMACY *123*

8. A NEW APPROACH TO THE REST OF THE WORLD: INFLUENCE . . *135*

9. LESS PARTISAN WARFARE, MORE REAL DEBATE *151*

10. DON'T FORGET THE BASICS: HAVE THE PATIENCE

TO REFLECT *163*

NOTES *175*

INDEX *179*

Show me a true patriot, and I will show you a lover not merely of his own country, but of all mankind.
—SCOTTISH PATRIOT ANDREW FLETCHER, 1707

To be ignorant of what happened before you were born is to be ever a child.
—CICERO

The way in which the world is imagined determines at any particular moment what men will do.
—WALTER LIPPMANN

LETTER TO A NEW PRESIDENT

Dear New President,

Each of the eleven Presidents I have known personally, from my favorite, Harry Truman, to your immediate predecessor, found himself standing before God on inauguration day, reciting the Oath of Office, hand on the Bible, and confronting the startling reality that no man or woman can ever truly be prepared for the awesome responsibility that now falls on your shoulders. I am quite certain that for a time at least, every new President must feel as humble and naked as Woodrow Wilson did his first night in the White House. Wilson, that irascible old idealist, held no inaugural ball, setting aside a tradition established by James Madison in 1809 on the grounds that he distrusted such "aggrandizement," and on his first night as an occupant of the White House, Wilson was startled to discover that the Presidential trunk had been misplaced and would in fact not be delivered until 1:00 a.m. Wilson went to bed that night "without benefit of nightclothes," as his biographer noted.

To cite my King James Bible, "Naked came I out of my mother's womb, and naked shall I return thither: the Lord gave, and the Lord hath taken away; blessed be the name of the Lord." (Job 1:21)

I hope that for you, too, the first night in the White House as President will be a deeply humbling experience. There will be time soon enough to learn what Thomas Jefferson had in mind when he spoke of the "splendid misery" of being President. I think you can do much worse than to emulate Gerald Ford, a man perpetually underestimated, who was never shy about looking to God for spiritual guidance, but also never made showy public displays of his faith. Ford was inaugurated on August 9, 1974, after Richard Nixon resigned, and told a traumatized nation that day, "Our long national nightmare is over. Our Constitution works." Ford marked his first night in the White House by kneeling and saying the same words he had recited nightly since he was a lad in Michigan: "Trust in the Lord with all thine heart, lean not on thine own understanding, in all thy ways acknowledge Him and He shall direct thy paths." (Proverbs 3:5–6)

John Adams was the first President to live in the White House, moving in on November 1, 1800, before work had even been completed on the lavish new presidential residence. The next morning, Adams wrote to his wife, Abigail: "I pray Heaven to bestow the best of Blessings on this house and all that shall hereafter inhabit it. May none but honest and wise Men ever rule under this roof."

Harry Truman was the greatest President in my lifetime, as I will explore further in this letter. He awakened on May 8, 1945, which was both his sixty-first birthday and his first morning at the White House as President, and at 9:00 A.M. went on the radio to announce that World War II was over in Europe. He called on the country to make the following Sunday a day of prayer. "The Allied armies, through sacrifice and devotion and with God's help, have wrung from Germany a final and unconditional surrender," Truman told a national radio audience.

"For the triumph of spirit and of arms which we have won, and for its promise to the peoples everywhere who join us in the love of freedom, it is fitting that we, as a nation, give thanks to Almighty God, who has strengthened us and given us the victory. . . . I call upon the people of the United States, whatever their faith, to unite in offering joyful thanks to God for the victory we have won, and to pray that He will support us to the end of our present struggle and guide us into the ways of peace."

We still need to be guided in the ways of peace. Pray now, and pray often, new President. Pray for success, yes, but pray also for our enemies. Pray for the likes of Iran's Mahmoud Ahmadinejad and Hugo Chávez of Venezuela, and pray for yourself that you may better understand such leaders and the forces that drive them. Pray every day that you may gain a deeper humility with every new crisis and challenge you face in office. Pray not vainly or to seek advantage, but pray with an open heart and an open mind. Recall the wisdom of Tolstoy, who said, *Love that in you which is in all of us and you will come one step closer to loving God.* A President not only must have a spine like steel and a mind that is always reaching for new insight and new wisdom; he or she must above all have a faith that is unerring, unfailing, and unbreakable, because that faith will be tested every day in the White House.

My own faith has been my bedrock since I was a boy growing up in the coalfields of southern West Virginia. I have a child's faith in God and, like President Ford, I say my prayers every night before I turn in, as I have since my early days in Wolf Creek Hollow, when the man and woman I thought were my parents instilled in me a deep respect for the Good Book's wisdom. Life in the mining camps in West Virginia was meager. My Mom was a stern, upright, religious woman who kissed me only once in her life. My Dad was the greatest man I ever knew and taught me every day by example the importance of humility and faith.

I learned back in Wolf Creek Hollow that it was a sin to believe that one was infallible. Not even Jesus Christ himself claimed to be infallible. We humans are mortal beings, wracked with the knowledge that we are forever doomed to fall short in our aspirations, but also forever soaring with fresh hope that we can create ourselves anew. This is the American story, the all-important chronicle of who we are, but nowhere, except in twisted mockery, is it ever claimed that we are incapable of making mistakes. If we saw ourselves that way, we would be claiming to be gods.

Any serious appreciation of the Bible reminds us that every person—and every President—must find the moral courage to take a hard look at mistakes made, so that he or she can learn from them. I have lived with the weight of my own youthful mistakes my whole life, like a millstone around my neck, and I accept that those mistakes will forever be mentioned when people talk about me. I believe I have learned from those mistakes. I know I've tried very hard to do so.

Only dictators and kings can get away with never having to admit their mistakes. The people will never trust you if you can't honestly admit your own mistakes. Harry Truman had a sign on his desk in the White House—"The Buck Stops Here"—and to him it was a way of life, not a slogan suggested by a slick spin man. John Kennedy was on the hot seat when the 1961 Bay of Pigs invasion of Fidel Castro's young communist government turned into a fiasco. Kennedy faced the fire. One cannot watch presidential news conferences nowadays without a shudder of unease to see how far these sessions have fallen since the old days when my friend President Kennedy ushered in the television age with his magnetic performances before the cameras. (President Eisenhower actually gave the first televised press conference, for you history buffs, on January 19, 1955; on January 25, 1961, President Kennedy held the first *live* presidential news conference in our history.)

Kennedy was eloquent and articulate and knew how to spar with a hostile reporter without short-changing the right of the American people to hear their President held accountable to the public. The press wanted answers during his Friday morning news conference on April 21, 1961, just one day after the failed invasion of Cuba turned into a propaganda bonanza for Castro and a black eye for the United States internationally. Kennedy fended off repeated questions about the Bay of Pigs, but did not shy away from taking full responsibility.

"There's an old saying that victory has a hundred fathers and defeat is an orphan," Kennedy said. ". . . Further statements, detailed discussions, are not to conceal responsibility, because I am the responsible officer of the government, and that is quite obvious, but merely because I do not believe that such a discussion would benefit us during the present difficult situation."

That kind of acceptance of responsibility must be the foundation for any administration that would endeavor to be respected and trusted by the people and, above all, to have the authority and legitimacy essential to the office of the presidency. It was a downfall of the George W. Bush administration that the President had such trouble ever admitting to a mistake, and in fact, made a great show of promoting officials who had badly botched their duties, instead of reprimanding—or firing—them.

Every new President, starting with you, should study the tape of the press conference Bush gave on April 13, 2004. Early in his presidency, George W. Bush made the perhaps understandable calculation that, given his misadventures with the English language, he ought not to engage in live give-and-take with the press, and proceeded to make himself less available for such sessions than any other President in history. He might have been wise to stick with that approach. Instead, his April 2004 press conference provided a moment that many historians will see as all too revealing.

Asked repeatedly about mistakes he had made in office, Bush balked. He had no answer for the question, as if he had never acknowledged to himself that he had made a mistake and therefore had never learned from his own missteps and false moves.

"After nine-eleven, what would your biggest mistake be, would you say, and what lessons have you learned from it?" Bush was asked by a reporter.

"I wish you would have given me this written question ahead of time, so I could plan for it," Bush said, and for some reason, most likely nervousness, some of the reporters actually laughed.

"John, I'm sure historians will look back and say, gosh, he could have done it better this way or that way," Bush continued, giving every indication of acting as if he were being forced to reply to an unfair, trick question. "You know, I just—I'm sure something will pop into my head here in the midst of this press conference, with all the pressure of trying to come up with an answer, but it hadn't yet."

For some, I suppose, the president's palpable awkwardness and unease in that moment came across as endearing human frailty. I beg to differ. The office of President demands certain standards of honesty and articulateness, and I would submit that a President who is unable to learn from his or her own mistakes, and then to articulate for a curious public what he or she has learned, is not prepared for that office. The public grows weary of perpetually being spoon-fed images of a grinning President greeting grinning supporters and talking incessantly about how great everything and everyone is. Leading a great country demands a deeper level of discourse, and it also demands a President able to use the mass media to make that discourse understandable to large numbers of people. The power of the bully pulpit must also be balanced by a deep regard for the manner in which it is used.

In *Dead Certain*, a book released in summer 2007, President Bush confessed to author Robert Draper that it "may be true" when people accuse him of "unilateral arrogance," a stunning admission. I truly do not know how to reconcile boasting about "unilateral arrogance" with President Bush's frequent mention of religion, which urges one to avoid unchecked arrogance for the evil it can unleash. Bush also told Draper that he did have a shoulder to cry on while in the White House: "Of course I do, I've got God's shoulder to cry on, and I cry a lot. I'll bet I've shed more tears than you can count as President," he said.

Yet none of that self-searching time spent with God seems to have mitigated President Bush's self-confessed "arrogance" or lent a hand in coming to terms with mistakes made. It was almost as if President Bush had read the Bible but somehow missed the most fundamental lesson emerging from the life and teachings of Jesus of Nazareth. That life is a testament to humility: Philippians 2:3–8: "Do nothing out of selfish ambition or vain conceit, but in humility consider others better than yourselves. Each of you should look not only to your own interests, but also to the interests of others. Your attitude should be the same as that of Christ Jesus: Who, being in very nature God, did not consider equality with God something to be grasped, but made himself nothing, taking the very nature of a servant, being made in human like-ness. And being found in appearance as a man, he humbled himself and became obedient to death—even death on a cross!"

It was almost as if President Bush were so worried about the public image of strength and decisiveness that he chose to con-struct for himself, he grew fearful of any mixed signal he might give. He obviously failed to heed the advice of that most Ameri-can of American writers, Ralph Waldo Emerson, "A great man is always willing to be little." It was almost as if his public image of toughness was all that George W. Bush came to value, more than the tens of thousands who have died in Iraq because of the war he unleashed or the thousands left homeless by Hurricane Katrina.

There is nothing particularly novel or unprecedented about investing so much in creating for the public a fictionalized, idealized political self, to which one must adhere at all costs; the peril lies in forgetting the fictionalized and idealized nature of this public self and giving it more power over one's conscience and actions than it deserves. The peril lies in snaring the public and the media in one's no-holds-barred effort to preserve the public image at all costs, including circumventing our laws and killing off true debate.

"[W]e can best understand the furies of war and politics by remembering that almost the whole of each party believes ab-solutely in its picture of the opposition, that it takes as fact, not what is, but what it supposed to be the fact," Walter Lippmann wrote in his classic 1922 study, *Public Opinion*. "And that therefore, like Hamlet, it will stab Polonius behind the rustling curtain, thinking him the king, and perhaps like Hamlet add:

> *'Thou wretched, rash, intruding fool, farewell!*
> *I took thee for thy better; take thy fortune.'"*

Mr. President or Madame President, this long letter seeks not to wade into matters of policy, but rather to explore deeper realities. (I wrote *Losing America* in 2004 to sum up how seriously I took the attempt of Bush and his advisers to undermine the Constitution in their pursuit of power for the executive branch, and I encourage you to read that volume as a companion to this. Neither, you will note, is a doorstop!) So in that spirit of deeper inquiry, let us look at "The National Security Strategy of the United States of America," a document issued by the Bush administration in September 2002, and consider it not as an exercise in policy, but as a warning about folly.

A year after September 11, our nation and its leaders were challenged to update strategic thinking and to grapple with the difficult choices that would come after the Afghanistan campaign. Boldness was required, along with at least a modest dose of reality. However, as a lifelong devotee of the wisdom of the Founding Fathers, I cannot imagine anyone who calls himself a U.S. patriot missing the central insight the Founders bequeathed us: that no one is above corruptibility and that, therefore, effective government requires an architecture that provides for ample checks and balances to guard against the abuse of power.

I would have thought every schoolchild could recite Lord Acton's famous dictum: "Power tends to corrupt; absolute power corrupts absolutely." No U.S. President can afford to forget those words, especially not since the end of the Cold War turned the United States into the world's most unrivaled world power since ancient Rome.

"If men were angels, no government would be necessary," James Madison wrote in "Federalist No. 51." "If angels were to govern men, neither external nor internal controls or government would be necessary. In framing a government which is to be administered by men over men, the great difficulty lies in this: you must first enable the government to control the governed; and in the next place oblige it to control itself."

As a man of faith, I have always seen my God as a figure for good. One cannot behold God and His magnificence without trembling at human frailty and human fallibility. We must kneel before His greatness. The lesson can never be lost that nothing man creates, man with all his flaws, can ever be free of the inevitability of flaw and imperfection. Yet some in the Bush 43 administration seemed to use faith as an excuse for believing they were on a divine "crusade"—Bush's highly unfortunate word choice—and that having God on their side guaranteed that whatever they did must be right.

Hendrik Hertzberg of the *New Yorker* magazine brought home this central error of the Bush administration in an October 2002 "Comment" piece that used as its starting point "The National Security Strategy of the United States of America."

Hertzberg, a one-time *Newsweek* correspondent who went on to write speeches for President Carter, noted that the sort of regime the Bush administration seemed to be extolling was, in essence, a police state. "The Bush doctrine's answer to this objection is essentially this: Hey, we're the good guys," Hertzberg correctly pointed out.

That, he went on to insist, can never be enough. Yes, we can certainly hope that people who share our values, such as our friends in Europe, will "embrace American hegemony" because they can expect us to use our great power to pursue positive goals, from "advancing democracy" to seeking to prevent terrorists from gaining access to more dangerous weapons. We can hope—but that hope only goes so far. We cannot possibly expect our friends or our rivals to believe that we will always use our power only toward the most noblest of objectives; to believe in such fantasy would be to dismiss countless centuries of human history.

"[W]hat a naïve view of power and human nature!" Hertzberg exclaimed in that "Comment" piece. "What ever became of the conservative suspicion of untrammeled power, the conservative insight that good intentions are not, are never, enough? Where is the conservative belief in limited government, in checks and balances? Burke spins in his grave. Madison and Hamilton torque it up, too. Are we now to assume that Americans are exempt from fallen human nature? That we stand outside history?"

The Bush years have taught us painful lessons about the importance of renewing our faith not only in God but also in the wisdom of the Founding Fathers in imbuing the Constitution with an elaborate and nuanced system of checks and balances. I believe in those checks and balances, and have devoted myself to deepening the tradition of Congress demanding its constitutionally mandated role in government.

Unlike some of my fellow Americans, I can say with conviction that I took no pleasure in watching as George W. Bush banished himself to the ignominious position of worst United States President ever. I truly wish it had not come to this. I had hoped to be able to take candidate Bush at his word in 2000 when he pledged to be a uniter, not a divider. I noticed his insistence that we must maintain a bedrock of humility in U.S. foreign policy. What impressed me at first about Governor Bush was what I thought was his dedication to his Deity. I thought a man ruled by strong religious faith would heed the message of the Good Book and be willing to look at himself and be pious, down to earth, and always humble. Nine years later, we all know it did not work out that way. Bush is a man who seems to be the center of his own universe. He seems to have learned little of human nature and even less of human history over his lifetime.

All presidents must struggle to remain humble, and they are not the only ones. I think it's hard for all of us in Washington to keep ourselves humble. I'm probably one who has not always succeeded in doing so, but in that lesson, too, comes humility. We all have a basic idea of what it takes to be a good President. We can argue about who was the greatest ever. George Washington was the Father of our Country and led us at Valley Forge when all seemed lost. There were no darker days ever for this country than those at Valley Forge. So he has to be number one. Thomas Jefferson was a great sage, a lot like John Adams, and I would also put Harry Truman in my top three, because of his courage and fidelity to his country. If you would have asked me what I thought of Truman in January 1953, as he was leaving office and I was arriving in Washington as a newly elected congressman, I would have told you that I did not like him too much. I have changed my views about President Truman over time. I learned from Harry Truman the virtue of being true to oneself and true to one's values. That's a lesson all of us in politics need to emphasize.

The study of even a little history (and I hope I can prod or inspire you to study much more than that) offers clear lessons about the qualities needed by a great leader. A President must have the confidence in himself to be as slow as he needs to be in coming to a decision; once he reaches that decision, he needs to be able to explain his thinking and convince others, and he must always continue to reevaluate his conclusions in light of subsequent developments.

The moments that define a presidency remain few, and the visionary chief executive keeps in mind the need to tune out the background noise and focus on going to the public—and the press—with honest arguments to build broad support for one's approach to acting on presidential priorities. Public support can thrive on rich and challenging dialogue or debate; enhanced public understanding can make the current of public opinion run deeper and wider and therefore harder to divert or diminish. The need for such dialogue and consent goes to the heart of a thriving, representative democracy.

"The democratic El Dorado has always been some perfect environment, and some perfect system of voting and representation, where the innate good will and instinctive statesmanship of every man could be translated into action," Walter Lippmann writes in *Public Opinion*.

Mankind was interested in all kinds of other things, in order, in its rights, in prosperity, in sights and sounds and in not being bored. In so far as spontaneous democracy does not satisfy their other interest, it seems to most men most of the time to be an empty thing. Because the art of successful self-government is not instinctive, men do not long desire self-government for its own sake. They desire it for the sake of the results. That is why the impulse to self-government is always strongest as a protest against bad conditions.

The democratic fallacy has been its preoccupation with the origin of government rather than with the processes and results. The democrat has always assumed that if political power could be derived in the right way, it would be beneficent. His whole attention has been on the source of power, since he is hypnotized by the belief that the great thing is to express the will of the people, first because expression is the highest interest of man, and second because the will is instinctively good. But no amount of regulation at the source of a river will completely control its behavior, and while democrats have been absorbed in trying to find a good mechanism for originating social power, that is to say a good mechanism of voting and representation, they neglected almost every other interest of men. For no matter how power originates, the crucial interest is in how power is exercised. What determines the quality of civilization is the use made of power.

What determines the quality of American democracy, dear President, is the use we make of our power. We have institutions in place to help this country avoid the misuse of power. Those institutions are Congress, the courts, and public opinion. The more we cut off true debate and exchanges of views, and let those in power use emotion, misdirection, and manipulation of truth to whip the nation into action, the more likely we are to make dangerous mistakes in how we use our power. A representative democracy only works when the people are involved. We need them. We are stronger and smarter in numbers, and it is only the power mad, intent on short-circuiting the Constitution, who fail to heed the wisdom of the people.

The notion of crushing any dissent or discontent with the direction of the government, before it can even be established whether that dissent or discontent is justified, principled, and honorable, could not run more counter to what our Founding Fathers believed ought to be the guiding principles of our republic. Those were, admittedly, vastly different times, when life moved at a slower pace and the acme of lethal force was represented by a musket or cannon, not the awesome mushroom cloud of a nuclear explosion or a bolt out of the sky from an unseen, unpiloted drone. Nevertheless, it is important to keep in mind the emphasis that no less a personage than Thomas Jefferson placed not only on dissent, but also on actual rebellions from time to time, if for no other reason than to keep leaders honest.

"God forbid we should ever be twenty years without such a rebellion," Jefferson wrote in a letter to William S. Smith in November 1787, before he had served as our nation's first Secretary of State or as our third President. "The people cannot be all, and always, well informed," he continued. "The part which is wrong will be discontented, in proportion to the importance of the facts they misconceive. If they remain quiet under such misconceptions, it is lethargy, the forerunner of death to the public liberty. . . . And what country can preserve its liberties, if its rulers are not warned from time to time, that this people preserve the spirit of resistance? Let them take arms. The remedy is to set them right as to the facts, pardon and pacify them. What signify a few lives lost in a century or two? The tree of liberty must be refreshed from time to time, with the blood of patriots and tyrants."

I chose to open this letter by emphasizing the importance of faith because I truly believe that the spirit of renewal and rebirth we so badly need to see encouraged in this country in the years ahead must start with a new moral seriousness, whatever an individual's faith, which can in turn lead us to deeper relationships with the other pillars of a democracy, the education of our young and the maintenance of a healthy and vigorous debate based on informed viewpoints, not name-calling. For me, as for so many others, my faith in the wisdom of the Bible enriched my faith in the power of ideas and in the power of knowing history and literature. One fed the other, and still does to this day. My faith also illuminates my study of science; nothing that Charles Darwin wrote contradicts the story of Genesis.

I stand with Ralph Waldo Emerson, who said, "All I have seen teaches me to trust the Creator for all I have not seen." I stand with that great genius of science, Albert Einstein, who said, "My religion consists of a humble admiration of the illimitable superior spirit who reveals himself in the slight details we are able to perceive with our frail and feeble minds." Yet to many, faith and learning are somehow at odds. The result is moral confusion. We all need reminders from time to time that all study of the wisdom of great books must be built on a solid moral foundation.

More than twenty-one years ago, a Chicago professor known for his translations of the classics published a book called *The Closing of the American Mind*. Allan Bloom was in effect setting off a loud alarm, and many readers resented the intrusion on their comfort with the status quo. Bloom was a conservative whose protégés include the execrable Paul Wolfowitz, and many dismissed him as a crank for his railing against the unruly, anything-goes mentality of so many who came of age in the 1960s. Despite the controversy, the book holds up well, and I hope you will include this daring and challenging meditation on your presidential reading list, whether you are reading it for the first time or the seventh. I find myself paying special attention now to the way in which Bloom argued that faith and moral education go hand in hand with the rigors of higher education.

"My grandparents were ignorant people by our standards, and my grandfather held only lowly jobs," Bloom wrote. "But their home was spiritually rich because all the things done in it, not only what was specifically ritual, found their origin in the Bible's commandments, and their explanation in the Bible's stories and the commentaries on them, and had their imaginative counterparts in the deeds of the myriad exemplary heroes. . . . Their simple faith and practices linked them to great scholars and thinkers who dealt with the same material, not from outside or from an alien perspective, but believing as they did, while simply going deeper and providing guidance. There was a respect for real learning, because it had a felt connection with their lives. This is what a community and a history mean, a common experience inviting high and low into a single body of belief."

As a lifelong Southern Baptist, I can find common ground with Bloom's description of his Jewish family life, as well as how he applies the importance of his upbringing.

I do not believe that my generation, my cousins who have been educated in the American way, all of whom are M.D.s or Ph.D.s, have any comparable learning. . . . When they talk about heaven and earth, the relations between men and women, parents and children, the human condition, I hear nothing but clichés, superficialities, the material of satire. I am not saying anything so trite as that life is fuller when people have myths to live by. I mean rather that a life based on the Book is closer to the truth, that it provides the material for deeper research in and access to the real nature of things. Without the great revelations, epics, and philosophies as part of our natural vision, there is nothing to see out there, and eventually little left inside. The Bible is not the only means to furnish a mind, but without a book of similar gravity, read with the gravity of the potential believer, it will remain unfurnished.

The challenge for you, new President, will be not only to use your faith as the fulcrum for your personal search for strength and resourcefulness, but also to talk of faith in a way that can bring people together, not drive them apart, as we confront our responsibilities as a nation. There will always be doubters and skeptics, cynics and psychoanalyzers. They can say what they want. We need to hear from our President about the ties that bind us. We need to be reminded that old-time virtues are no less virtuous merely because they have stood the test of time or because we live in a period in which a short attention span has come to be seen almost as a goal to be pursued instead of a shameful shortcoming.

When I invoke the importance of faith in exploring where we as a country are headed in these pivotal times, I am not talking about marketing religion for profit or politics. No, I am talking about a faith that is searching and potent, challenging, and above all humbling. That faith must be the anchor that holds and the mast to which one can cling against the storms. Faith can never be used as an excuse to run off half-cocked on misbegotten adventures, justifying any mistakes in advance on the ground that as a believer, all is permissible because of good intentions. History, that cold-eyed muse of mine, takes a savage glee in highlighting the foolishness of any who would thumb his nose at her many warnings about the certainty that good intentions are never, ever enough. As the philosopher Karl Popper wrote in 1945, "The attempt to make Heaven on Earth often produces Hell."

To me, we are living through times in which faith and trust are under siege. Too many Americans have lost their trust in the representatives they send to Washington, who often slip into a routine of spending much of their time raising money for their next campaign rather than grappling seriously with the issues of the day, and too often fall into a narrow partisanship that trades on attack, and values only victory. Too many Americans have lost faith in the fundamental honesty and truthfulness of their leaders in government.

It is true that a certain number of Americans are able to see through the attempts to train them, through relentless repetition, to believe in the inartful obfuscation and blatant manipulation that has emanated from even the President and the Vice President, but I would submit that not nearly enough of our citizens are equipped to do so on a consistent basis. A growing cynicism and loss of trust are eating away at the foundations of our republic. People tune out, eyes glazed, and pass their time with the amusements of popular culture, forgetting for the moment the responsibility of each and every citizen to help drive the Ship of State. Our system, based on the consent of the governed, cannot long survive if the people can succumb so easily to manipulation and misinformation.

Too many Americans have lost faith in—or are just plain ignorant of—the wisdom of our Founding Fathers and the system of government they envisioned. Like faith in God, faith in the Constitution and in our form of government must constantly be updated and revisited, and it must be fueled not by fear, but by hope. I never thought I would live to see a day when the fearmongers had come to so completely dominate American life, as other, cruder fearmongers had come to power in Italy and Germany during the first third of the twentieth century. Our weakness for fear will never completely leave us, of course. There will always be those who find advantage in playing to the weaknesses in all of us. I am more vexed by those who would purport to be patriots but would look to sell America short.

I have noted with alarm over the years a disturbing trend: The more superficially our leaders understand our history and the historical realities of other countries, the more willing those same leaders are to manipulate the people and the more easily they get away with selling extreme conclusions to the public based on fantasy, not reality. Ronald Reagan is remembered as a strong leader, in part because he cultivated that image, and in part because his decisions as President played a role in bringing an end to the Cold War. There is danger, however, in forgetting that a central aspect in much of Reagan's thinking was an almost pathological fear of the Soviet Union.

It was good and proper to have a healthy regard for the power of the Soviet state and to make sure that our citizens remained vigilant and alert about the need to match strength with strength. I was considered for many years a leading advocate of a muscular foreign-policy approach to the Soviet threat. During the Carter administration, I flew all the way to Soviet General Secretary Leonid Brezhnev's dacha in the Crimea to disabuse him of the notion that as Senate Majority Leader, I would be party to simply rubber-stamping the Strategic Arms Limitation Agreement (SALT II) that President Carter had negotiated with Brezhnev. That 1979 trip gave Brezhnev no room to doubt the toughness and seriousness of the Congress in facing off against Soviet expansionism.

But for Reagan, legitimate concern about Soviet intentions veered wildly toward the irrational. He not only harbored feverish, nightmarish visions of the Soviets as some kind of superhuman rivals; he also tried to scare people into adopting his stunted view of the world. Twenty years before he became President, Reagan gave a speech to the Phoenix Chamber of Commerce in 1961, and said, "One of the foremost authorities on Communism in the world today has said we have ten years. Not ten years to make up our minds, but ten years to win or lose— by 1970 the world will be all slave or all free."

Even as President, Reagan continued to express lurid visions of our country being overrun by communism; he talked about the "red tide" that would be lapping at the shores of Harlingen, Texas. What that meant to most people at the time was that we could expect hordes of communists to swarm up from Latin America and, presumably, overrun the United States, just as Reagan had warned they might in that 1961 speech. For some reason, some who embrace what they call conservatism constantly pander to public fears of weakness and humiliation. They will not admit to the overwhelming strength of the United States and its people, apparently not understanding that anxiety politics hurts this great country.

What possible good could come from telling the world that the United States was so weak that we could easily be overrun by our enemies? The end of the Cold War brought home the stark truth that the Reagan-era claims of U.S. weakness were absurd. Our military was strong. Our fighting men and women were strong. Our will to prevail was strong. This business of crying "Wolf!" in order to gain cheap political advantage has undermined the quality of our national dialogue. This is a dangerous trend we must all confront together.

American political leaders need to be calmer and more precise, both when we are dispensing good news and bad news. Leaders need to be patient, consistent, and eloquent in our public explanations. Only that approach, over time, will compel more people to stop ignoring politics, elections, and even political discussion as so much white noise. Nothing is more toxic to a healthy national dialogue about where we are and where we are going than the lazy habit, grown now to epidemic proportions, of denying potentially ominous developments even in the face of over-whelming evidence. Fie on thee! Most certainly only a fool with little knowledge of the past embraces the simpleton's notion that things will continue to roll along just as they always have. Yet in most political commentary, the cries of alarm that should be loud and clear over the basic assault we have witnessed on our Constitution in recent years have been muted far too much. The misguided notion has gained ground that a bland complacency is understandable or acceptable even in the face of the inescapable truth—which deep down each of us must know—that eternal vigilance will always be required to preserve liberty.

The United States has just emerged from one of the gravest national crises in our 233-year history, and we are going to have to start thinking as a nation about lessons learned if we are finally to get on the road to recovery. One of George W. Bush's most grievous failings was the extent to which he acted as if he were the President of only that small portion of the country that voted for him and continued to support him, and that everyone else was somehow un-American and rude if they declined to give him unconditional love and support.

You, dear President, are the President of every single American. You are the President of Barry Bonds and Rosie O'Donnell. You are the President of the poet and the dreamer and of the accountant and the meter maid. You are the President of the commodities trader talking on his cell phone in a crowded glass elevator near the top floor of the latest jagged tower to emerge in Manhattan, and you are the President of the tech-support operator in Arizona waiting for the Manhattan commodities trader to stop shouting. You are the President of hordes of unkempt liberals, some of whom look as if they were on their way to a 1960s-themed costume party. You are the President of paranoid billionaires puffing on their cigars right now, staring at footage of you, their new President, rolling over and over again on cable news, and asking themselves what else they can do to undermine your presidency, beyond all the stunts and tricks they have most likely already pulled to try to stop you from leading the country forward.

Whether you are a Democrat or a Republican, and as I write these words I cannot know which party has prevailed in the elections, you will have been bombarded with negative attacks in all manner of publications, and through radio and Internet, so much so that you cannot help but carry a certain bitterness. A new President does not suddenly stop feeling the prodding of human nature. However, as one who has suffered the slash-and-burn attacks of ugly politics, I know that you have also been given an unbelievable opportunity. Should you go on the attack and focus on retaliation, no one would be surprised. If, however, you can make it your personal mission to bring alive the teachings of faith in a meaningful way for the life of this nation, so that we can begin to heal the divisions through common brotherhood and understanding, you have the opportunity to make a huge contribution to the epic task of restoring American moral standing in the world and to generating a new national conversation in which discretion and thoughtfulness might find a foothold among the warring factions of politics.

I do not know how many years I have left, or even if I will still be among the living as you read these words I've labored over here in my ninetieth year, for my state and country, but I will say this: If you are looking for partners in an effort to help us build a new era of national healing, I am ready to join you, and to enlist the help of a few friends here in the United States Senate and many more back home in West Virginia, too. We need to put our people back to work on the job of rebuilding the faith of the citizenry in their government. This is what they want to do. They want their belief restored. They are weary of doubting their leaders. The people want to be inspired, not whipsawed by fear and manipulation. They want to be able to hope again.

I do not envy you, new President. We cannot begin to encourage other countries to see us again as a friend and ally, rather than a raging monument to the dangers of power-grabbing monomania, until we start at home with a fundamental reassessment of who we are, how we fit into the world, and what our responsibilities and obligations are to work constructively with the rest of the world on such problems as nonproliferation and global warming. The people of Europe are involved in a decades-long discussion about their future, and now face such critical choices as whether our NATO ally Turkey, which shares a border with Iraq, should become part of the European

Union. That discussion in Europe has been loud and noisy at times, and no one would see it as a model. But it reminds us that once the curtain has been pulled back on the myths of the Bush years, when fear was used to quiet discussion, and incompetence was perpetually celebrated to spur unquestioning loyalty, one has every reason to believe that the return of freedom of thought and freedom of discussion will be like a breath of fresh air. I certainly hope so. We have a lot to discuss and debate.

Make no mistake: We need our friends abroad just as much as they need us. In fact, we may need them *more* than they need us. The number-one danger of power is its ability to corrupt, and the way it does so is first to convince the powerful that they no longer need to pay much attention to how they are perceived by others. Even worse, it teaches the bad habit of disregarding even cogent and spot-on advice from friends and allies, if that advice does not support the direction that yields ever more power. That, however, is the dark side of power—power as an end in itself, not a tool to be applied judiciously to real-world problems.

I am still waiting to hear some of my colleagues in Congress step forward before the TV cameras and apologize for the thoroughly vicious and mule-headed things many of them said about our friends in Europe in the months leading up to the Iraq War. I have never been completely at home in the Washington social whirl. I'm just a boy from West Virginia, raised poor and proud, and I've never been one to try to pile up friends. I would rather have a few close friends than many who call me friend but do not show it. More than anything, I value the persons close to me who will tell me the truth, whether I want to hear it or not.

Oddly enough, George W. Bush showed in a September 2004 interview with *Time* magazine that he seemed aware of the vital need to avoid cocooning himself with yes-men. "If I were interviewing a guy for the job of President," Bush told reporter John F. Dickerson, "I'd ask, 'How do you make decisions? How would you get unfiltered information? Would you surround yourself with hacks? Are you scared of smart people?' I've seen the effect of the Oval Office on people. People are prepared to come in and speak their minds, and then they get in there, and the place overwhelms them, and they say, 'Gee, Mr. President, you're looking good.' I need people who can walk in and say, 'Hey, you're not looking so great today.' "

Our friends in France and Germany, mindful of the history that unfolded on their continent in the last century, saw it as their role to raise principled objection to the case for war in Iraq as it was being presented by the administration. Defense Secretary Donald Rumsfeld was flying high in February 2003. He was getting everything he wanted, and other than a few critical speeches here and there, including some by me in the Senate, and some wise Internet and radio commentary, Rumsfeld had mostly transcended criticism. Secretary of State Colin Powell went before the United Nations on February 5 in what has now become universally seen as a low point in an admirable man's career. Powell, called on to make the case for war by twisting intelligence, trotted out a duct-taped bundle of odds and ends, from mobile trailers to falsely identified aluminum tubes. No one should have been persuaded by that for a minute, least of all Powell himself. Yet at the time war hysteria raged like a hot wind. I knew of a few war proponents who had deeply held views behind their position, but the vast majority went so over the top in making calm discussion impossible, their excess will forever burn as a kind of national shame.

Three days after Powell's speech to the UN, Defense Secretary Rumsfeld flew to Germany to participate in the 39th Annual International Security Conference in Munich and found himself getting an earful from the German foreign minister, a former 1960s radical named Joschka Fischer.

"My generation learned you must make a case [for war], and excuse me, I am not convinced!" the German foreign minister shouted in English, looking right at Rumsfeld for effect. "That is my problem. I cannot go to the public and say, 'These are the reasons,' because I don't believe in them."

The question Fischer kept raising about the plans for war was "Why now?" and neither Rumsfeld nor anyone else had a credible answer.

"No one wants war," Rumsfeld insisted. "War is never a first or an easy choice. But the risks of war need to be balanced against the risks of doing nothing while Iraq pursues the tools of mass destruction."

Doing nothing? We knew right there the man was delusional. I'm not fond of name-calling. I don't mean that in an ad hominem sense. I mean it quite literally: Rumsfeld had slipped into the realm of delusion, and expected others to join him there. Let us remember that at the time, a team of United Nations weapons inspectors was on the ground in Iraq, looking for weapons of mass destruction. The simple truth about these UN inspectors was that, despite what one might have heard, they were effective, very effective. In fact, here's a remarkable fact to chew over: UN arms inspectors were responsible for destroying more weaponry in Iraq in the years after the Gulf War than the U.S. military destroyed during the war itself.

No one who was not being whipped up into a state of fear by the likes of Rumsfeld and Condoleezza "Mushroom Cloud" Rice could begin to comprehend the administration's argument that it was somehow dangerous to debate the rationality of a war that could hurt the United States for generations to come. Bush and Rumsfeld were actually claiming that we could not afford to wait even long enough to let the arms inspectors finish their job, and reacted harshly when challenged on the baselessness of their arguments.

Three days after the conclusion of that conference in Munich, I gave a speech on the Senate floor. "On this February day, as this nation stands at the brink of battle, every American on some level must be contemplating the horrors of war," I said. "Yet, this Chamber is, for the most part, silent—ominously, dreadfully silent. There is no debate, no discussion, no attempt to lay out for the nation the pros and cons of this particular war.

There is nothing. We stand passively mute in the United States Senate, paralyzed by our own uncertainty, seemingly stunned by the sheer turmoil of events."

What we needed to be doing at that time was to be listening to vastly differing arguments about the basic assumptions of the plan to go to war. Joschka Fischer offered every Senator a chance to snap awake and take a longer view than merely counting the number of months that had ensued after the horrific September 11 attacks.

Pardon an aging Senator for quoting himself a bit more to sum up where I thought we stood at that critical historical juncture:

This Administration has turned the patient art of diplomacy into threats, labeling, and name calling of the sort that reflects quite poorly on the intelligence and sensitivity of our leaders, and which will have consequences for years to come [I said in that speech on February 12, 2003]. Calling heads of state pygmies, labeling whole countries as evil, denigrating powerful European allies as irrelevant—these types of crude insensitivities can do our great nation no good. We may have massive military might, but we cannot fight a global war on terrorism alone. We need the cooperation and friendship of our time-honored allies as well as the newer found friends whom we can attract with our wealth. . . .

To engage in war is always to pick a wild card. And war must always be a last resort, not a first choice. I truly must question the judgment of any President who can say that a massive unprovoked military attack on a nation which is over 50 percent children is "in the highest moral traditions of our country." This war is not necessary at this time. Pressure appears to be having a good result in Iraq. Our mistake was to put ourselves in a corner so quickly. Our challenge is to now find a graceful way out of a box of our own making. Perhaps there is still a way if we allow more time.

Five weeks later, the Iraq War was under way. Six years later, we look back on the fevered retreat from responsibility that characterized the buildup to war, and it is now clear that the points the angry and unyielding German foreign minister raised in Munich have already been ratified by history. Our friends in France and Germany were telling us what we needed to hear, not what we wanted to hear, and we have never forgiven them.

So please, new President, I hope that you will give a speech soon in which you outline the need to have allies that think for themselves and have their own ideas on how to continue to build the strength of international alliances and institutions. I urge you to give a speech thanking our allies for being the kind of healthy, prospering democracies that insist on a vigorous airing of different views. I urge you to remind Americans and people in other countries that under your leadership, this country will never again be so arrogant as to think it can merely dictate its worse impulses and force everyone to go along with them.

That will be a controversial speech, but so be it. No President I admire has ever shied away from a challenge and I know you will be no exception. One test of our national seriousness in getting down to the hard work of reviving our political culture, making the fearmongers and demonizers pay a price for un-American Machiavellianism, will be whether we can truly redefine ourselves internationally. The tradition of American democracy is special and unique not because we are loud in proclaiming it such, but because that tradition, although forged in a much different historical period, has proudly stood the test of time and successfully responded to the many crises in our republic's history. To rebuild U.S. diplomatic credibility in the world may require decades. The trick will be to have something to say to the rest of the world that does not sound either patronizing or bullying, like so many of the ugly pronouncements heard during the George W. Bush years.

I know you can do it, new President. I hope I will be around to watch you restore a balance so long lacking in our national life between, on the one hand, tough-minded self-interest with a minimum of self-delusion, and on the other, a deep and abiding respect for the tonic effect of openness and honesty. Your duty will be nothing less than helping us as a country to know again what it means to be Americans, an unruly bunch at times, oh yes, always, and not necessarily of one mind or one heart on even the most vital issues and problems of the day, but a land nonetheless dedicated to pluralism and inclusion, not to Orwellian rule over a dispirited majority by a small, determined minority of extremists.

I write this letter as a man shaped over the years by the experience of war and peace, by partisan truculence in Washington,

and by hard-won periods of relative bipartisanship and har-
mony. That history teaches caution when it comes to the longing
for an unattainable paradise of a country in which our national
discussion and our politics are blissfully free of even a hint of
rancor or unpleasantness. I had enough of fairy tales as a boy
back in Wolf Creek Hollow.

No sensible person ever claimed that representative democracy is perfect. All systems of government have their flaws, and
our form of government has always been and always will be an
ongoing experiment. It is, in a sense, an unlikely house of cards,
though it has been built on a solid foundation, emerging from
generations of development of culture and civic and political institutions. Aristotle wrote, "It is evident that the state is a creation of nature, and that man is by nature a political animal.
And he who by nature and not by mere accident is without a
state, is either a bad man or above humanity." Yet it is also wise
to keep in mind the warnings of many others, such as Bertrand
de Jouvenel, who quipped, "A society of sheep must in time
beget a government of wolves."

Those who would advertise their dedication to bringing
change to Washington must heed the first lesson taught by our
own political history and that of the world: No individual, other
than God, can truly claim to be a master of that genie we call
change. Those who stumble blithely forward bolstered by blind
faith in the power of their good intentions are certain to find
themselves in turn mastered by change and its tidal currents,
not the other way around. We are all, each of us, human and

fallible, and in our efforts to bring change, the only certainty is that the change we might help unleash will never and *can* never be exactly the type of change we think we have sought. We can be certain only that the unforeseen, unimagined consequences of that change may well surprise us.

The state of California has often seemed a sort of national petri dish. Trends and fads are often introduced there and begin their evolution toward national phenomena or they go nowhere and are soon forgotten. Back in 1978, two men in California named Howard Jarvis and Paul Gann campaigned for Proposition 13, a statewide measure that would put almost a freeze on property taxes. The initiative was controversial, but managed to pass with 65 percent of the vote, stirring up a national fever of tax cutting that, like most fevers, ran its course on its own terms and in its own time frame with no regard for what might have been expected of it.

Ronald Reagan's last two years as governor of California reduced his standing in the eyes of many, but out of office in 1978, he seized on Proposition 13—once it had passed. Senator Richard Schweiker, then a U.S. Senator from Pennsylvania, told a gathering in Philadelphia in June 1978, the same month the measure passed, "I believe that Proposition 13 is the cause that will propel Governor Ronald Reagan all the way to the White House in 1980." Reagan vowed before the same gathering that he would try to do just that, using Proposition 13 to light a "prairie fire" of opposition to "costly, overpowering government."

The practical effect for Reagan was that he was off and running as a tax-cutting crusader and would be elected President on the promise of being fiscally prudent and then proceed to run up record budget deficits. The practical effect for California was that its once-great educational system, which relied on property taxes for funding, had to slash its budget and lay off talented, committed young teachers with a passion for education. Many of the best teachers were forced to find other jobs. Within a few years, California schools went from being ranked number one nationally in student achievement to as low as forty-eight out of fifty in some surveys. Change, once it begins its march, can sweep forward long past whatever limits or controls we might naively believe will naturally govern it.

The man or woman of action does not need to adopt a willful blindness in order to stride forward into the arena, determined and unflinching. A deeper knowledge of what men and women have endured and overcome in similar times of trial does not hinder the capacity for action, it enhances it. Does anyone imagine that George Washington was in any sense unaware of how close our young nation was to annihilation during that long winter of horrors at Valley Forge? Franklin Roosevelt was not a champion of massive social programs like the Civilian Conservation Corps and the Works Progress Administration, which did so much to help the nation through the grim and trying years of the Great Depression, a miserable time that I experienced firsthand; no, FDR was above all a champion of optimism and its first cousin, experimentation, and he kept putting himself on the line during those dark days, trying whatever new approach might show a glimmer of hope until World War II truly brought us out of the Depression.

Ronald Reagan, for all his actor's love of Manichaean shades of black and white, branded the Soviet Union an "evil empire," but he never became a captive of his own rhetoric. In the summer of 1986 he capped off years of preparation and travelled to Reykjavik, Iceland, for a crucial summit with the reforming Soviet leader Mikhail Gorbachev armed with an intense desire to take bold steps toward peace, up to and including trying to abolish all nuclear weapons. History is an enemy to those leaders who mock and disdain it, believing they can arrogantly stand astride it armed only with the wish that all will turn out as they hope; but history, though severe, treats as friends those leaders who have arrived at an awareness of her vicissitudes and contradictions, especially when it comes to that most solemn of choices any leader must make, the decision to go to war.

We can never enter into one war without making sure we remember the lessons of previous wars. That does not mean we merely keep in mind the talking points or fictions that have been presented to rewrite history; it means striving ever to come closer to an understanding of war in all its facets, its madness and depravity, its rapacity and sadness. President George W. Bush gave a speech in August 2007 that attempted to make a case that the legacy of the Vietnam War somehow argued for sending more men and women to die in Iraq in a war we could not win. Historical blindness on that scale deserves analysis, and I will devote a section of this letter to the lessons of history, but for the time being I would like to focus first on the most important war of my lifetime, World War II.

I worked as a welder during the war at shipyards in Baltimore and Tampa. To men and women of my generation, American involvement in the world at that time was a given. We watched the GIs storm the beach at Normandy and fight all the way to Berlin. We gritted our teeth through the Battle of the Bulge, where nineteen thousand Americans fell, and rejoiced in V-E-day and V-J-day. Most of all, though, when the dust of war cleared, we looked to these lands ravaged by war and asked ourselves tough-minded questions about what to do next.

We Americans were smart enough at that time to understand that our victory against the National Socialists was in and of itself not a major accomplishment; no, only if we could do our part in helping the survivors of war build new countries from the ashes of their destruction would our victory in war truly become meaningful. We must reteach our people the lessons of what we have learned. They can gain not only wisdom but also hope by looking with a fresh perspective at the challenges we've faced down in the past.

We destroyed Germany in order to save it. Failure was not an option in the fight against fascism in Europe and the Pacific. The world had never seen anything like the bombardment we inflicted on the cities of the Reich, and Berlin after the war was no longer a city, but an obscene landscape of destruction. As a bright young writer, Andrei Cherny, explores in a new book, *The Candy Bombers: The Untold Story of the Berlin Airlift and America's*

Finest Hour, an essential and inescapable truth of the twentieth century is that the United States was never closer to all-out war with the Soviet Union than in the tense days of the Berlin Airlift in 1948. Harry Truman understood what few others did that year: If Berlin fell to the Russians, the entire continent would fall behind the Iron Curtain.

Gail Halvorsen, the original candy bomber, looked down on the wretched waifs, starved by war, who converged around the Berlin airfield where he regularly landed his cargo plane, and saw not hateful little Nazi spawn, but children. Soon he was dropping chocolate bars from the sky. To make sure the candy would not hit too hard and explode on impact, he raided his supply of handkerchiefs to fashion small parachutes, and Berlin's children quickly learned to watch for him. This one American, dubbed "Uncle Wiggly Wings" by the young Berliners and later joined by many others in the candy-bomber campaign, helped us hold out during the seemingly impossible days of the Berlin Airlift, when the Soviets were trying to starve an entire city's population to force us to abandon Berlin to them. This one American, with his big heart and belief in treating children like children, helped us set Germany on the road to democracy. As Cherny's exhilarating account makes clear, this was one that could very easily have gone the other way.

> [T]he face-off in Berlin would be the closest the United States and Soviet Union ever came to World War III. After the Berlin blockade, the conflict between the Americans and the

Soviets settled into a dangerous but somewhat stable balance of terror. As Paul Nitze, the [Secretary of Defense James] Forrestal aide who went on to be a foreign policy adviser to seven presidents, would write in 1999, "I still consider the Berlin crisis of 1948 to be the most parlous moment for America, far closer, in my view, to drawing us into conflict with the Soviet Union than the later Cuban missile crisis."

But despite the danger, Truman's policy of avoiding both aggression and appeasement worked. Before the blockade, Soviet Communism had been a force that was on the move, creeping across the map of Europe and toppling free governments one by one. After the blockade was defeated, the Communists would not gain another inch of territory in Europe. In fact, they would never again even try. . . . Though no one knew it at the time, the victory of the Airlift would mark the sunny apex of the American Century—before the slow slog of Korea, before the shock of Sputnik, before Americans had even heard of places such as the Bay of Pigs or Khe Sanh.

I worry about an America in which plenty and comfort have turned us into spoiled children who take it as a given that life should be easy and free of pain and suffering. The King James Bible I keep right next to my desk in the offices of the Senate Appropriations Committee speaks of famine and pestilence; it tells version after version of the same tale, which is that we discover our humanity in times of turmoil and tragedy. Yet when the levees broke in New Orleans in August 2005 after Hurricane

Katrina made landfall in Louisiana, it was as if the poor of that region were not our brothers and sisters, but lepers or outcasts, whose misfortune and agony earned them not compassion and a commitment to meaningful help, but ostracism and stigmatization.

The boondoggle of President Bush choosing to fly over the stricken areas in the immediate aftermath, rather than going down and taking a look for himself, was first of all a failure of, if not common sense, compassion. This son of privilege and dynasty who had defined himself as the President of only that fraction of the country which shared his worldview was incapable of seeing that he must do his best in that time of tragedy to be one with the people. The scandal of his frat-boy bonhomie with the then already disgraced Federal Emergency Management Agency (FEMA) director, Michael Brown—when he told him, infamously, "Brownie, you're doing a heck of a job"—was the jagged break with reality such banal good cheer represented in the face of tragedy. It was the willful and purposeful distancing from truth of a man who lived in a bubble, as was instantly clear not only to the residents of the Ninth Ward in New Orleans, hurting and traumatized, but to people everywhere in those parts of the country where not everyone lives in protected gated communities.

It was hard not to wince when Barbara Bush, the president's mother, remarked that the Katrina refugees who had been crowded into the Astrodome in Houston, and eventually resettled elsewhere in Texas, were probably better off and, by implication, should be grateful at this upgrade in their circumstances, not

haunted at the memories of losing their homes and their communities.

"So many of the people in the arena here, you know, were
underprivileged anyway, so this—this is working very well for
them," she told a radio station.

To a world that had often been appalled at troubling evidence of how callously the United States, the richest nation in
the world, handles its poorer citizens, Barbara Bush's oblivi-
ousness was telling. The *Economist* magazine in Great Britain,
never thought of as quick to criticize the United States, published a searing cover story the month after the disaster, titled
"The Shaming of America," which looked to the tragedy—and
its woefully mishandled aftermath—as evidence of dry rot cor-
roding the American system. The magazine noted that the
American image abroad has always commanded respect, even
among our enemies, because of the can-do spirit we have
shown so often before. We might be seen at times as "arrogant,
overbearing, and insensitive," the magazine observed, but, by
God, we can get things done. That perception of us shifted noticeably after Hurricane Katrina, however. The disaster "ex-
posed some shocking truths" about us, including the divide
between black and white, the deterioration of our physical in-
frastructure, and "the abandonment of the dispossessed," the
magazine wrote, concluding, "But the most astonishing and
most shaming revelation has been of its government's failure to
bring succor to its people at their time of greatest need."

One year after the disaster, the BBC looked back at how the

international reaction had unfolded and observed: "New Orleans is in a struggle over how it will be rebuilt—and whether the poor and working-class African Americans who made up a large part of its pre-flood population will ever be able to return. Race, class, money and power are inextricably linked in the U.S., and the flooding of New Orleans is proving a textbook example of how they intersect."

No one among us can heed the lessons of Jesus Christ in every aspect of our lives, but we can try. We can set our goal as endeavoring mightily, day in and day out, to do just that. Of all the biblical tales that I have found myself returning to again and again over the years, few have as much power as the story of Jesus and the leper: Luke 5:12 "And it came to pass, when he was in a certain city, behold a man full of leprosy: who seeing Jesus fell on his face, and besought him, saying, Lord, if thou wilt, thou canst make me clean."

The tableau of human existence is the interchangeability of affluence and want, of triumph and depredation. The one is the flip side of the other; neither can exist without its complement. That is why the only way to honor the stable and prosperous American society we built in the decades after World War II is to remember, always, how close we remain to Hobbesian chaos. The moment we grow blind to that duality, and all that it tells us about ourselves, we have baited a trap for ourselves with potentially disastrous consequences. No leader can guarantee the nation will avoid hardship. No leader can promise victory in a war or struggle too massive to be confined to one administration.

We must of necessity take the long view, and I have never backed away from believing we as Americans must think big and dream big; that does not mean, however, that any President is more than the successor to whoever held the job before him or her, or the precursor to whoever comes next; working in concert, looking to build something in tandem with other leaders, is the only way to accomplish that which is truly important.

I started out on a long journey of discovery as a boy, finding in histories of Rome and of the Founding Fathers essential tools to knowing who I was and what I wanted to work for in representing the people of West Virginia in Washington. I may have had something to prove, I will readily admit, if not to my colleagues in the House and then the Senate, then at least to myself. I craved a deeper knowledge of our republic and its traditions the way a hungry man craves bread.

Over the years, as my love of reading took me deeper into an understanding of what had previously seemed mysterious, the character of my reading changed. I read more for pleasure and less for edification, or the pleasure I took in edification outstripped any sense of duty or obligation I might have had in immersing myself in the wisdom of Cato the Elder or marinating in the particular accomplishments of the ancient Etruscans. I sought respite from the rigors of legislating in the cool wisdom of books because the heroes I found there were my teachers and companions. Other Senators used legislative recesses to take ski trips or chase cash donations. I went home to West Virginia to visit with constituents and hear what was on their minds, the way I always have been eager to do, and on the way I reread books like *Robinson Crusoe* by Daniel Defoe and the works of Ovid and Shakespeare.

To me, these were adventure stories, and the best of adventure stories at that: those that started with a thorough view of human nature, neither jaundiced nor naïve, and focused on one more iteration of the classic human struggle to battle our baser elements and find dignity and identify good. Such stories have no impact in a sanitized bubble where bland self-satisfaction and prosperity are seen as ends in and of themselves, never as a means to finding a deeper, more meaningful life. If we do not heed, always, the horrible missteps that humanity has made and will make again, the failures and catastrophes of history and the damage that has been wrought will mean nothing to us. If we gloss over what we can learn about humanity in the most appalling of times, then we have no guide for how to face future disasters.

That is especially true when we confront that most horrific of legacies in all of human civilization, the terrible crimes against humanity conducted by the Third Reich when so many millions of Jews and other so-called enemies of the Reich were rounded up and murdered. I agree with anyone who would urge all of humanity to adhere to the moral imperative of "Never again!" and if we cannot agree on that, we can agree on nothing. However, I fear that the moral urgency of "Never again!" may be trickier than many imagine.

We can never settle for skimming off a few cheap lessons from World War II, but must forever search for new insights into how Hitler's victims found it in themselves to fight back toward a sliver of redemption in a world that must have looked to them like hell on earth. A friend recently told me a story about Berlin in those spectral years after the war when residents of that city were continually on the edge of starvation. So many Jews had been killed or hounded into leaving the country that the city's large and thriving prewar Jewish community had dwindled to but a few. These were lost souls, individuals who had seen far too much of horror and senseless cruelty. They had no reason to believe in anything, least of all God, and many were ready to leave Hitler's former capital and never come back.

That is what the few remnants of Berlin's Jewish community would most likely have done if not for brave souls like Estrongo Nachama. Classically trained as a tenor in his native Greece, Nachama survived Auschwitz and the grisly Death March that followed. Nachama had a golden voice. To hear that voice was to see sunshine and hope. One could not help it. Nachama began to sing twice a week for the Jews of Berlin in the one synagogue that had not been destroyed in the war, and slowly more and more began to come out to hear him. He was direct in his appeal: If you can't believe in God anymore, he told people, come for my voice.

Nachama kept singing in Berlin beyond his eightieth year, and this was how *The New York Times* marked his death in January 2000: "Estrongo Nachama, the chief cantor of the Berlin Jewish community and the man who did as much as anyone to revive Jewish life in the city after Hitler destroyed it, died on Thursday. He was 81. . . . Vigorous to the last, eyes always glimmering, his voice scarcely affected by age, Mr. Nachama exuded the passion for life of a man who had seen the worst horrors and come through. He was an Auschwitz survivor, spared because his voice pleased the SS guards, who particularly enjoyed his rendering of 'O Sole Mio.' "

I do not have a voice that can fill an auditorium, and few do. No matter how dangerous and difficult a time we face now as a country, it can hardly compare to what the Jews of Europe faced during the war and in its aftermath. But I believe strongly in attending to the lessons of history not only when they are grim and oversized but also when they are subtle and easy to miss. When it comes to the legacy of one of our most important achievements as a nation, defeating the Hitler evil, we seem to have missed the lesson.

The principled objection of Germany to the Iraq War was more than anything a validation of U.S. values. We tried to build democracy upon the embers of war, knowing it would take generations to see if we could be successful, and it was only when Germany became whole again, following the fall of the Berlin Wall in 1989, and began to stand on its own that we could see if that effort to implant democracy from without, always a highly uncertain undertaking, had truly taken hold. It had. Our friends in Germany had learned their lessons well.

I believe we must bear in mind two main aspects of this great historical lesson. The first is that we must bring music— and good cheer—to our effort to communicate with the public.

I would never have gone anywhere in politics if I couldn't fiddle. I would drive the backroads of West Virginia in my early years of campaigning and show up in a small town where I knew almost no one. I am not naturally a gregarious individual, but I always brought my fiddle and had a whale of a time performing tunes like "Sally Goodin" and "Arkansas Traveler." The people appreciated enjoying some down-home music before we ever got to the political talk, and they always gave me a fair hearing. That's all you can ever ask for: a fair hearing.

If you offer people something, if you reach out to them and don't just use them like pawns, your chances for a real dialogue are much better. It will always be true that if the people can't relate to you on some level, they won't hear what you have to say to them. Grim as the Bush legacy is, opportunity now hangs in the air. We can make great strides in this country as we come out of the fog of government by fear and generate a time of healing to remind ourselves of who we are. Every political discussion does not have to feel like a trip to the dentist's office. We can find new ways to engage and inspire the public.

The other lesson is that it takes time to build the things that most matter. We built our tradition of democracy through more than two centuries, only to have our Constitution weakened during the last eight years. Those who tear down the work of generations in a self-serving frenzy need only a handful of years to wreak their havoc. Those of us who would build back our legitimacy must think instead of decades and centuries, not mere news cycles.

I would scold some of the campus theorists of various political stripes who argue that American power and influence in the world are certain to wane precipitously. Of course it will wane, but only over time. To quote Ecclesiastes: "To everything there is a season, and a time to every purpose under the heaven: a time to be born, and a time to die . . . and a time to kill, and a time to heal; a time to break down, and a time to build up."

I have watched a young nation suffer through a Great Depression that robbed men and women of basic dignity. I have witnessed the grim sense of expectation that hung in the air as the American people solemnly mobilized for a war in Europe that we knew we might not be able to win. I have seen us becalmed in periods of national malaise and unsure of ourselves in times of national scandal. Through it all, I have never doubted that the people would in the end elect leaders to see us through the dangerous times, and repair the damage done in times such as the past eight years.

I know that you understand the nearly epic importance of the challenge that faces you in the next four years, new President. I know that you do not need to hear from me or from anyone else to be reminded of the need to strive always for a deeper and wiser base of humility, and to find new ways to challenge your views and give voice to internal arguments before a decision is reached. What I hope, dear President, is that I am echoing many of your own concerns and prescriptions in this letter, but that in doing so I can offer a soupçon of support and encouragement. I seek not to change your mind about anything, but rather to put to work a sampling of my perspectives, which may in a quiet moment cheer you up or calm you, bring a smile to your face or a timely frown.

When I talk in the pages ahead about the need to learn from history—or to view an effective press as an asset to democracy, not an impediment; or to shake up our whole view on why we need to have friends in the world and can't afford to go it alone—I am talking out loud, in a sense, sharing my thoughts as background music. I hope mine will be one of many books that help us to form a new consensus not only on who we want to be as a people, and a nation, but how we want our President to represent us. We can't avoid a national dialogue about what leadership we deserve, in all senses, and what our stake as individual citizens is in investing our democracy with the creative energy and critical attention of our people as a whole. So here's to you, new President, and here's to giving people new reason to be proud of their country.

1. BRING BACK THE FIRESIDE CHAT

I t is no accident that in recent years we have heard precious few references to a man who was without doubt one of our greatest presidents, Franklin Delano Roosevelt, that brave leader who told a shaken and dispirited nation that the only thing we had to fear was fear itself. Truer words have never been spoken. Only a fool claims to be a stranger to fear, and of course one can never move completely beyond fear. As Mark Twain wrote, "Courage is resistance to fear, mastery of fear—not absence of fear. Except a creature be part coward, it is not a compliment to say it is brave."

Nor, however, can an entire nation be held hostage to fear week after week and month after month and year after year without paying a catastrophic price. The American people and, yes, all too many of their political leaders have been manipulated and controlled in recent years through the most shameless use of fear that this country has ever seen. Sadly, and shocking as it must be to stare down so sobering a reality, even the infamy of Joseph McCarthy's reign of demagoguery in the 1950s did not threaten the Constitution as directly as what we have endured of late.

Now is the time, new President, for us to strive to move beyond fear as a national obsession and a national paralysis. We need to look to FDR's wisdom for guidance not only because he was the longest-serving President in our history, a captain who steered our ship of state through treacherous waters during the Depression and rallied the nation to fight the forces of tyranny during the Second World War; but we must also look to Mr. Roosevelt, to his integrity and to his eloquence, because he was above all a man of privilege who had a heartfelt understanding of the common man. If we cannot have a President from the wrong side of the tracks, with all the hard-won life knowledge that background inevitably entails, we can at least demand a leader with more than the blinkered vision of the complacently well off. Roosevelt was capable of the loftiest ideals and rhetoric, but always sought to address his words to the commonsense wisdom of the cop walking the beat or the schoolteacher in a one-room classroom in Nebraska or, yes, the grocery-store butcher in a small town in West Virginia. FDR never condescended to the people, and he was honest and direct in a way that puts the most recent administration—and anyone associated with it—deeply and indelibly to shame.

This is no time for sweet talk or mincing of words. We must face the stark truth that our nation now faces a crisis as deep and dangerous as any in our proud history. That crisis is not the threat posed by a small band of zealots hiding in mountain caves and brewing up an incoherent cocktail of hate and resentment against us. The people have always been smart enough to understand that no outside force, save that which would literally wipe us from the map with untold megatonnage of nuclear weaponry, can ever undermine the basic fabric of our democracy and our social order. Only we can do that.

If nothing else good comes from these last eight years, it can at least be hoped that every citizen will come to understand that we can never take our values and our principles for granted and that we must constantly reaffirm and rearticulate them, not only for ourselves but also for the world. We must be ever vigilant against homegrown forces that would turn a nation founded on the universal rights of man into one now internationally identified as willing to torture, willing to hold people behind bars with no charges filed, willing to justify almost any extreme action on the basis of a highly warped and irrational view of the world. Our political leaders must be ever wary of the true dangers confronting the nation, but it has become sadly apparent that the most pronounced dangers we face are the forces that threaten this country from within. These pose a much more immediate and corrosive threat than anything that Osama bin Laden and the hundreds of faces of terrorism can ever hope to accomplish from without.

One cannot help but hold an alarmist view of what has happened to this country since September 11. Where does the cycle of fearmongering and scaring people end? It is very fine to say that we must do better than to resort to using fear in the political

realm, but it is the rare politician who can refrain from resorting to a tactic of such proven effectiveness. For the foreseeable
future, it's likely that pushing the buttons that make people
afraid will continue to be a tactic of all too many politicians.
This is, in short, a time which begs for true leadership. Some political leader with great reserves of courage must step forward
and have the audacity to be straight with the people, and declare
that we cannot continue to worry about terrorists under the bed
every time we pick our head up off the pillow. I hope that leader
of courage and vision will be you, new President.

So let us now look to the example of the leader who helped
show the American people a way through the darkest days of the
twentieth century, a man who began his presidency with an un-
forgettable inaugural speech that I would humbly suggest you
might consider citing in your own first inaugural address. If I
may try my hand at setting the scene a bit, to those of us who
lived with FDR as a true political icon, it's worth recalling that
even before he had given his first major speech as President,
expectations were already high. The week before his pivotal
address, *The New York Times* published an article under the
headline ROOSEVELT SPEECH EAGERLY AWAITED; CAPITAL HAS
NEVER SO ASSIDUOUSLY SOUGHT A FORECAST OF AN INAUGURAL
ADDRESS. Arthur Krock reported: "Not in years, if ever before in
this country's history, have the words of a President's inaugural
address been so prayfully awaited as those which Franklin D.
Roosevelt will utter next Saturday. Never before perhaps, in the
week before his inaugural, has a President-elect been under

such pressure to anticipate the address he will make after taking the oath."

Even as a fifteen-year-old lad in Stotesbury, West Virginia, I could not help but be aware of the sense of expectation in those dark days of the Depression, and Roosevelt did not disappoint when his time came on March 4, 1933. "I am certain that my fellow Americans expect that on my induction into the Presidency I will address them with a candor and a decision which the present situation of our people impel," a stern-faced FDR began, and I can think of no other words that would be more appropriate for the present.

"This is preeminently the time to speak the truth, the whole truth, frankly and boldly," he continued. "Nor need we shrink from honestly facing conditions in our country today. This great Nation will endure as it has endured, will revive and will prosper. So, first of all, let me assert my firm belief that the only thing we have to fear is fear itself—nameless, unreasoning, unjustified terror which paralyzes needed efforts to convert retreat into advance. In every dark hour of our national life a leadership of frankness and vigor has met with that understanding and support of the people themselves which is essential to victory."

New President, that support is what you as well must ask from the people. I do not worry that we as a nation may have begun to feel we have lost our innocence. As a young lad I studied David Saville Muzzey's *An American History,* which began with the grand statement, "America is the child of Europe." No one would now term America the child of anyone. We are, for better or worse, lumbering toward middle age as a country, and our youthful pride in the rightness of our ideals and our traditions has uneasily given way to doubt. We have, as too often happens beyond the first flush of youth, lost our optimism. Such is the risk of greater experience. As Mark Twain tartly put it, "The man who is a pessimist before forty-eight knows too much; if he is an optimist after it, he knows too little."

Franklin Roosevelt, uncommon spirit that he was, gave the lie to that humorous quip. No one would ever accuse FDR of knowing too little and yet he was a man who fairly burned with optimism and humanity. His was a voice capable of speaking to life's truths without resorting to mere sonorousness or false wisdom. In that same inaugural speech he also observed, "Happiness lies not in the mere possession of money; it lies in the joy of achievement, in the thrill of creative effort. The joy and moral stimulation of work no longer must be forgotten in the mad chase of evanescent profits."

Most important of all, FDR reminded all of us, including those of us listening to our radios in West Virginia coal country, of the foundation of our great traditions. "Our Constitution is so simple and practical that it is possible always to meet extraordinary needs by changes in emphasis and arrangement without loss of essential form," he counseled, and again, the words bear repeating now. "That is why our constitutional system has proved itself the most superbly enduring political mechanism the modern world has produced. It has met every stress of vast expansion of territory, of foreign wars, of bitter internal strife, of world relations."

Only the hijacking of democracy during the Bush years has succeeded where no other challenge in our nation's history could have: We not only cannot take our Constitution for granted any longer; we must actively seek to restore its place of honor in our national life and look to bring back what it has always represented to the entire world. It will not be nearly enough merely to refrain from doing further harm; to accept the trajectory on which the previous administration has placed us is to court danger. That is why the time has come to go to the people and enlist their creativity and good sense in these extraordinary times and put it to work for the good of the country.

We can only move past the numbing damage of recent years if we seek a new kind of consensus not only about the problems we face, but also about how to solve them and how to prevail. Huge percentages of the population tell pollsters in poll after poll that this country is on the wrong track. It's up to you to reach out to them and reteach them a sense of possibility and yes, optimism. I don't believe we as a country are ever going to be beyond optimism. Sometimes it's hard to do. All we know is that Bushism can't last.

Just eight days after the resounding success of his inaugural address, Roosevelt once again gave a memorable talk. This time, the President was addressing the nation through the new medium of radio in a folksy, down-home talk which he decided to call a "Fireside Chat." "My friends, I want to talk for a few minutes with the people of the United States about banking," he said in that first of what turned out to be a series of thirty wildly successful speeches, usually on Sunday night, always to massive, rapt radio audiences. In conclusion, FDR declared, "You people must have faith; you must not be stampeded by rumors or guesses. Let us unite in banishing fear."

To you, new President, and to others who were taught about those speeches in schoolbooks, they might seem merely like a tired anachronism. They might seem as if they have little to do with the realities of a world in which seemingly everyone walks around with small gadgets chirping and hiccupping and demanding their attention at all hours of the day and night. We now have the tools to call up whatever fact or piece of trivia might seem useful at the time, and are awash in too much information ever to sit back and have a clear thought, so it must be hard for some to imagine the idea of an entire nation waiting in repose for the familiar voice to come on the radio, leaning forward toward the console and staking so much, so very, very much, on the sound of each and every word.

But for me it requires no act of imagination. I was there. I know that a leader can imbue the people with optimism because I saw it in the faces gathered before the radio for those Fireside Chats. As a boy, I witnessed firsthand how just hearing the sound of that reassuring, resonant voice saying "My friends" lifted people's spirits and gave them hope. As a boy, listening to FDR, I felt a new day dawning. The integrity and humanity in that voice were so strong, I just believed him, and so did everyone else. The people needed that jolt of optimism the President gave them, and that need—and its fulfillment—was what made FDR so beloved a figure. One could step into any little coal miner's home down there in West Virginia and you would see a picture of Franklin Roosevelt. He was more than a President.

FDR's genius in holding a series of talks meant to evoke the fireside atmosphere of a conversation between friends or family members does not necessarily translate well to our more cynical age. Presidents have for years been giving Saturday radio addresses, but these have as much in common with Roosevelt's eloquent, searchingly composed addresses as a form letter from a national political party has with a handwritten love letter. We need to have both the humanity and risk of the FDR talks returned to our national life. We need to hear our President reaching out to the people, starting a real dialogue, not just steamrolling through a speechwriter's catalog of ludicrous hype, such as one Bush speech from October 2007, which had the temerity to insist, against all available evidence, that the worries of so many Americans about the economy were in fact misplaced. "This is an historic time for our nation's economy," the President droned, tone-deaf to the concerns of real working people.

Any real dialogue must be built on a true commitment to honesty, a quality in which, sadly, all too few of our leaders excel, and it must include a willingness to tap into the public mood. The same technological tools that leave most Americans overloaded and short-circuited can be used to do the hard work of building consensus around a new direction and new energy in the pursuit of the priorities that so many Americans share. But it is not nearly enough only to reach out and build support for major priorities of your new administration, whether they be working to give every American access to health care or designing innovative new programs to help working people build for their retirements.

We are talking about the soul of the nation. Nothing less is at stake. Toward that end, we are in dire need of a new call for belief and hope, a new animation of that great American trait of wanting to lend a hand. John F. Kennedy, for his inauguration on January 20, 1961, finished his first speech as President by memorably imploring Americans to dare to think big. "And so, my fellow Americans: Ask not what your country can do for you—ask what you can do for your country," he said. "My fellow citizens of the world: Ask not what America will do for you, but what together we can do for the freedom of man. Finally, whether you are citizens of America or citizens of the world, ask of us the same high standards of strength and sacrifice which we ask of you. With a good conscience our only sure reward, with history the final judge of our deeds, let us go forth to lead the land we love, asking His blessing and His help, but knowing that here on earth God's work must truly be our own."

These are the themes that must be revivified and restored. To regain access to our own better natures, rather than the angry delirium of a country stung by an attack we have spent far too much time reliving, will require faith and courage. It will require bold and daring new approaches to communication. If that means venturing out and about in the country, visiting a room full of schoolchildren to give one national address, or a gathering of firemen to give another, that might be a good start. The good citizens of this country have had enough of the embarrassment of a President so reduced in credibility, so shrunken in public esteem, that he dare not venture out to speak to truly representative groups of Americans, only those that were selected under the most controlled of circumstances.

The American people crave a leader who can throw open a window and let in the sunshine and light. They yearn for a President who can gain strength and focus in hearing diverse perspectives. They demand a leader who can see challenge not as a threat to his own tottering legitimacy, but part of the essential give-and-take of representative democracy. Above all, they require a national figure that can treat them with dignity and honesty and trust them to understand the real problems of this nation and the world, not merely cook up fanciful scare schemes like those in the latest Hollywood blockbuster to come rolling into the neighborhood movie theater with its millions of dollars of special effects. Leave aside the flimflam, and look to the good in every American. You will not be disappointed.

2. TEACH THE PEOPLE ABOUT
THE CONSTITUTION

ear new President, I have been lucky enough in my life to have had two great passions that always have given me at least as much back as I have given them: my love for my wife of sixty-nine years, fair Erma, and my absolute reverence and regard for that masterpiece of a political document, the United States Constitution. Its words still ring for me with the clear beauty of truth, and in its parchment pages I can still find fresh wisdom and guidance welling up as excitingly as they did when I was a boy in Wolf Creek Hollow reading by kerosene lamp about the ideas of those men who led us through the Revolutionary War period and the birth of a nation.

My belief in their foresight and wisdom has been the pole-star that has guided me through my fifty-six years in Washington as a congressman and Senator. For as long as I can remember, I have made a habit of more at all times carrying with me in my front pocket a copy of the Constitution, consulting it often and without hesitation. I suggest you do the same, new President. After what it has been through during the two terms of your predecessor, it needs the attention.

We live in times of devalued patriotism. People say they love this country when what they mean is that they love the way they think it makes them sound to keep talking about how much they love it, without ever showing that love in any deep or meaningful way. How can we talk of loving our country if we seem to know ourselves less well all the time? How could those in power have leaned hard on rhetoric about patriotism even as they either took part in the dismantling of the great institutions of this country or stood by passively and watched the damage proceed apace? How could they adopt a pious, holier-than-thou tone in almost every pronouncement and self-justifying explanation when they have trampled on the Constitution and dishonored the brave visionaries who built this country?

Patriotism must be a heartfelt and joyous expression, not a reflex. Americans stand upright at sporting event after sporting event, staring off at an electronic version of the U.S. flag rippling on the big scoreboard as a pop singer of the moment sings yet another ad hoc version of "The Star-Spangled Banner." That is all well and good. I have always been an admirer of Francis Scott Key, and I recommend that everyone, at one point or another, visit Fort McHenry in Baltimore, where the tattered flag made it through the night. Our anthem rightly stirs patriotism in all our breasts, but it is, one must acknowledge, not a deeply searching exploration of what it means to be an American. We have that in our most important document.

Our Constitution is not a flower that wilts over time. The values and insights it contains remain always fresh, and I hope, new President, that you will embark on a major effort to reacquaint the American people with our founding document. I understand that memorization as a tool in education may have come in and out of favor more than once since I was a boy, but in the case of the Constitution, I would insist at the very least that each and every citizen be able to speak out loud, at a moment's notice, the great Preamble. I would like to hear a cacophony of voices, some deep, some high-pitched, some tuneful, some stammering, bringing the words to life with fresh conviction and fresh attention. This would truly be music to my ears.

"We the people of the United States . . ."

That is a simple beginning, but also important: the *people* of the United States, referring to all of us, every citizen, not just those who have their hands over their eyes and believe any rationalization presented to them by a power-hungry President.

". . . in order to form a more perfect union . . ."

The Framers were not men who dropped words in by accident. They thought about every word. They argued about every word. When they wrote "more," it was there for a reason. The reference was not to a "perfect union." That was never the claim, and can never be the claim. Our goal has always been a "more perfect" union, an improvement on previous systems of government, absolutely, but not a system that would ever claim the arrogance of being perfect, of being without flaw, of being beyond scrutiny or skepticism.

". . . establish justice . . ."

Our national ideals call for us not to "boast of" justice, or "take it for granted," but to *establish* it. This must still be our goal. We have, as we all know, regressed in this department in recent years.

". . . insure domestic tranquility, provide for the common defense, promote the general welfare . . ."

It's all right there, before our eyes, the directive that government *be* government, that it provide services to the people, not that it outsource these responsibilities and in the zeal to privatize end up lining the pockets of wealthy contributors turned defense contractors or security consultants.

". . . and secure the blessings of liberty to ourselves and our posterity . . ."

The blessings of liberty, a lovely phrase which to my ear conveys an essential point, that liberty is not an entitlement, not something ever to be taken for granted or to grow complacent about; it is, rather, a blessing, "a thing conducive to happiness or welfare."

". . . do ordain and establish this Constitution for the United States of America."

Hear, hear!

It is perhaps understandable, even inevitable, that for many Americans, the tone and spirit of these words would ossify over time, but that was never the intention of the Founders. They were smart, learned men with the sense of high and noble purpose that comes with the installation of knowledge, the great scope of history, where our nation fits in. They saw the Constitution as a document that would have continuing relevance to future generations precisely because it was put down as a marker at a key juncture in the road not only for the American people, but indeed for all of mankind. Thomas Jefferson, uniquely eloquent and perspicacious even by the standards of his peers, saw this better than most.

"It has been frequently remarked that it seems to have been reserved to the people of this country, by their conduct and example, to decide the important question, whether societies of men are really capable or not of establishing good government from reflection and choice, or whether they are forever destined to depend for their political constitutions on accident and force," he wrote in "Federalist No. 1," the opening salvo in that great reflection on democracy, *The Federalist Papers.* "If there be any truth in the remark, the crisis at which we are arrived may with propriety be regarded as the era in which that decision is to be made; and a wrong election of the part we shall act may, in this view, deserve to be considered as the general misfortune of mankind."

The same can be said of the disrespect for the Constitution that ran rampant under your predecessor. It was truly to the general misfortune of mankind that our basic freedoms were eroded so dramatically. President Bush signed an executive order declaring a national state of emergency on September 14, 2001, and every single year subsequently he quietly extended the state of emergency forward, long after the initial shock of

September 11, so that he could more easily continue to scorn and dismantle the constitutional protections we hold dear.

I was invited in April 1998 to give an address on the Constitution to a distinguished gathering at West Virginia University in Morgantown, and began by citing the results of a recent poll, which found:

- 91 percent of respondents agreed with the statement "The U.S. Constitution is important to me."
- Yet despite that figure, only 58 percent understood that the Constitution established the three branches of our federal government, the executive branch, the legislative branch, and the judiciary.
- Only 66 percent knew that the first ten amendments to the Constitution represent the Bill of Rights.
- Only 58 percent knew that nowhere does the Constitution proclaim that "the first language of the United States is English."
- Fully 85 percent mistakenly thought the famous words "All men are created equal" appear in the Constitution, or simply did not know where they are inscribed.

It will always be true that if you don't know what you have, you will not appreciate it. If Americans do not even see the ground on which they are standing, they will trip and fall and open the way for unscrupulous leaders to thwart their will. In recent years, no insult has inspired greater dread among those in Congress—and anywhere else in the country where principled objection has arisen to Presidential power running amok—than the epithet "soft on terrorism."

This was how *The New York Times* summed up the dynamic in October 2007: "As the debate over the eavesdropping powers of the National Security Agency begins anew this week, the emerging measures reflect the reality confronting the Democrats. Although willing to oppose the White House on the Iraq war, they remain nervous that they will be called soft on terrorism if they insist on strict curbs on gathering intelligence."

That was the story again and again, even as polls showed Republicans losing their edge in public perceptions about fighting terrorism as the evidence of incompetence and mendacity piled up all around. But I would like to take a step back and ask: Shouldn't the ultimate insult to be flung at an opponent in the political realm be the charge not of being soft on terrorism, a transparently self-serving accusation, but of being soft on the Constitution? What could possibly be more damning?

The Patriot Act was an abomination whose nomenclature was deeply steeped in the naming tradition laid out by George Orwell in *1984,* where the "Ministry of Truth" was anything but. That cursed act called for spying on untold millions of Americans, monitoring what library books they checked out, listening in on the private conversations of people who happened to have spoken with someone else who popped up on a surveillance list, and on and on and on, deep into what had for so long seemed inviolable territory in this country.

Winston Smith, Orwell's main character in *1984*, has the job of rewriting historical documents at the "Ministry of Truth," based on the latest party line, and it is a demanding task. Every day, he is given a new party line and must rewrite accordingly, even if today's line is the opposite of that of the day before, which in turn was the opposite of the day before that. " 'Who controls the past,' ran the Party slogan, 'controls the future: who controls the present controls the past,' " Orwell writes.

We can never allow our historical documents to be rewritten. Any who would try are the worst sort of hoodlums and charlatans and, yes, fools. What September 11 should have represented to us was not an excuse for permanent war, for unleashing perpetual fear into the lives of Americans, but a time to take stock as a nation and reflect on our better selves. September 11 should have been a time to give thanks to the greatness of the Constitution, because it is that noble document which gives us our strength. It is that noble document which arms us with the determination and balance and courage to find our way through any crisis. With the Constitution as our shield, we need never be a nation gripped by fear.

I have heard many facile comparisons in recent years between the United States, unprecedented world power that it has become, and the Roman Empire, whose famous fall teaches caution about the sustainability of hegemony. We are less like Rome than many people seem to think. We ought to spend less time worrying about becoming the new Rome and more time seeking to emulate the Romans. Each and every President takes an oath of office, standing before God and man and making a pledge to support and defend the Constitution, and so does each and every member of Congress. An oath is neither a formality nor an empty vestige of past practice; it is, instead, an essential act of self-definition and faith.

To the Romans, an oath was sacred, never to be violated, even when given to an enemy. A Roman would die—literally die!—if he had taken an oath to do something and could not do it. Yet too many of our national leaders take an oath and seem to forget it as soon as the words have passed their lips. New President, if I can ask of you one small favor, not for me but for the people we both serve, I beg of you that today, your first in office, when you take that solemn and miraculous oath to uphold our wise and wondrous Constitution, you will commit every fiber of your being to honoring it and heeding it just as insistently as any Roman would.

3. NO LIFE STANDS
OUTSIDE OF HISTORY

e must study the great figures of our history and carry them forward in our imaginations as living, breathing presences we can in effect consult on vital issues of the day. I wonder if even one in one hundred Americans has any idea where Greensboro, North Carolina, gets its name. I wonder if even one in 100,000 does. The answer, of course, is that North Carolina's third largest city was named for Nathanael Greene, hero of the Revolutionary War. Greene started as a private, but in 1775 became a general and ultimately rose to a stature second only to General Washington himself. An unlikely military leader, Greene was a Quaker from Rhode Island who walked with a limp noticeable enough to make him the target of frequent ridicule. His rise owed everything to meticulous study of military history. For years he had been devouring such volumes as *Instructions to His Generals* by Frederick the Great of Prussia and Julius Caesar's study *The Conquest of Gaul.*

"Study to be wise and learn to be prudent," Greene wrote to a young friend when he himself was but thirty. "Learning is not virtue but the means to bring us an acquaintance with it. Integrity without knowledge is weak and useless, and knowledge without integrity is dangerous and dreadful. Let these be your motives to action through life, the relief of the distressed, the detection of frauds, the defeat of oppression, and diffusion of happiness."

Those are vitally important words to bear in mind in these times of knowledge and integrity having fallen into such short supply. I have described how as a boy I read about the great figures of the Revolutionary War period, but in that pantheon Nathanael Greene early on earned a special place in my esteem. I memorized the entire chapter about Greene in my primer and took to heart the lesson of his life: that with hard work and deep study, a man can improve himself and equip himself to fight in the great battles of his day in a manner that can bring honor to both himself and his country.

"In becoming one of the Continental army's greatest soldiers, Nathanael Greene personified the power and potential of the new American idea—especially its rejection of the Old World's aristocratic governments and equally aristocratic military commanders, and its embrace of merit and virtue as society's ultimate arbiters," Terry Golway wrote in *Washington's General: Nathanael Greene and the Triumph of the American Revolution.*

"Indeed, during Greene's long service from the war's beginning to its triumphant and unlikely end, this self-taught amateur fought many bitter battles against two symbols of the Old World: [Lord Charles] Cornwallis, a professional soldier, and

Baron Wilhelm von Knyphausen, a commander of mercenaries who knew no loyalty other than to war. These opponents, who fought Greene in New York, New Jersey, Pennsylvania, and the Carolinas, represented all that the American Revolution opposed: inherited power, unearned titles, and imperial militarism."

As a young nation we arrayed ourselves against mercenaries and power for power's sake, and I see no reason why, moving in on two and a half centuries later, we cannot hold fast to those guiding principles. We have become addicted as a nation to the sensation of change. We look upon the surface of things and see in the shimmering and shifting light of the moment patterns that we tell ourselves are profound. But such glimpses are at best unedifying and at worst misleading. The deeper truth, visible with time and study, is that the decades—and centuries—of our national history resemble one another more than they differ, and it follows that the same can be said of ourselves in this history-adverse era and the great figures who people our history. As Mark Twain put it, "We are all alike—on the inside."

A decade before the September 11 tragedy was exploited for partisan political gain by those who, like children facing a new challenge for the first time, wail that everything has changed and nothing can ever be the same again, an influential writer published a widely remarked-upon essay called "The End of History and the Last Man." Francis Fukuyama's tract, first published in book form in 1992, was a serious attempt to grapple with the tides of history, specifically looking at where the world—and the U.S.'s place within it—was headed in the years after the 1989 fall of the Berlin Wall and the end of the Cold War that it represented.

In the original version of the essay, published in *The National Interest*, Fukuyama argued, "What we are witnessing is not just the end of the Cold War, or a passing of a particular period of postwar history, but the end of history as such: that is, the end point of mankind's ideological evolution and the universalization of Western liberal democracy as the final form of human government."

This was an interesting and serious argument, relying in part on Fukuyama's close reading of Hegel, and it is true that many misinterpreted the argument or took it too far. Too many people were in the dark after the end of the Cold War—an event none had seen coming, and so none could now explain clearly—and felt a reflexive desire to match the epic importance of so major a lurch forward in world history with sweeping pronouncements.

Fukuyama later did an about-face and asserted that his famous argument was not in fact valid, offering as justification for this change of heart—in *Our Posthuman Future: Consequences of the Biotechnology Revolution*—the caveat that if human nature changes over time, as he was arguing it did, then one could not speak meaningfully of an end to history. "The more science tells us about human nature, the more implications there are for human rights, and hence for the design of institutions and public policies that protect them," he concluded.

I would advise strong caution, new President, in falling into the trap of believing that human nature changes over time. To cite Ecclesiastes,

What has been is what will be,
and what has been done is what will be done;
there is nothing new under the sun.
Is there a thing of which it is said,
"See, this is new"?
It has already been,
in the ages before us.
The people of long ago are not remembered,
nor will there be any remembrance
of people yet to come
by those who come after them.

The events that shape our lives are but a reflection and reiteration of the many events that have shaped the many lives that have come before us. Lord Bryon spoke of history having only one page because it repeats itself, and because human nature does not change. There is no denying that Byron was correct. It takes a curious form of arrogance to blind oneself to that inescapable truth. I learned that much back at Mark Twain High School in Stotesbury, and I find it almost impossible to conceive that George Bush and the people around him, many of them armed with advanced Ivy League degrees, would not accept a certain humility about the truth of history.

History is going to be wary indeed of what we did in our time. We have lost our way. We have lost our sense of responsibility and our sense of our own past. We don't want to be great, because we don't think we are great, and to reclaim our way we have got to be thoughtful of history. That is the key not only to seeing the present more clearly, but also to raising criticisms within a larger context. If one has a good sense of history, there will be a respect for historical institutions and a corresponding effort to edify them, not to tear them down.

I cannot for the life of me understand how so few people seem to remember how high the stakes were during the Cold War. Early in my time in Washington, during my years as a congressman, I was part of a delegation that traveled to Nevada to witness a nuclear explosion. I have never forgotten the tension in our bunker as we waited for the blast. We knew we were well protected by untold layers of lead. We knew every precaution had been taken. But we were of a generation that remembered all too well the shocking carnage of Hiroshima and Nagasaki, not in some slide-show history-course sense, but in a dizzyingly visceral sense. We knew that, with the snap of the fingers, a whole city could suddenly be incinerated. We sat and waited for that explosion, wondering what it would be like to be so close to all those hydrogen atoms dying painful deaths as they created new helium and released energy. Then we were told the surprise news: no go. The test had been scrubbed. Like the Cold War itself, our trip to Nevada ended with a whimper, not a bang. But that does not mean we did not understand and live with a terrible presence in our lives.

I was considered stubborn in some quarters and eccentric in others when I flew to the Soviet Union in 1979 to meet with Soviet Premier Leonid Brezhnev in my role as Senate Majority Leader. I went to reinforce upon him the constitutional importance of giving the Senate ample time to thoughtfully review an important nuclear-arms treaty of the day, SALT II. Brezhnev and his klatsch of yes-men had no idea what a Senator Majority Leader did. In their system such an officeholder had all the importance and respect of a janitor. But not in our system! I flew *Air Force Two* as far as Leningrad, and could not have been more surprised when our Soviet hosts told me I was expected to fly Aeroflot down to Yalta for my meeting with the General Secretary. For those of you fortunate enough never to have heard of Aeroflot, the Soviet airline, it was legendary for having more crashes than any other airline, not to mention the roughest takeoffs and landings around.

I declined their offer.

"No," I told the delegation they sent to greet me at my hotel. "I want a special plane. I'm the leader of the Senate."

This was step one in my lesson about coequal branches of government. They were disappointed and talked tough, but I didn't budge. I asked them, "Would you expect a top Soviet leader visiting America to go on just any U.S. passenger plane?" No, one would expect him to have a plane that has the equipment befitting his work—not necessarily his style, but what he represents, what he is. I think they expected me to back down and were surprised when I held firm. They were noticeably uneasy as they left to go back to Moscow to explain my recalcitrance on this point to party leaders.

When they came back to Leningrad they were all smiles. They had good news for me: Brezhnev was sending his private plane to fly me down to his Black Sea dacha. That was quite a ride. Inside the plane there was nothing but red. I mean that literally. Everything was red: the tablecloth, the seats, the walls, even the dress of the hostess. The plane landed in the Crimea and we boarded a helicopter, which touched down on a beautiful hilltop. I looked out and there on the lawn was Brezhnev. As he rose to come over and speak to me, I saw he was reading a book. We went inside with our two interpreters and had a direct, nononsense talk. By the end we had reached an understanding: I drank a toast to him, and he toasted me, too. Brezhnev understood that he must respect the role of Congress and give us time for thorough consideration of the treaty.

It is not enough to have merely a passing knowledge of history's great dramas and personages. To know that Hitler and Stalin were the two most notorious figures of the twentieth century might be enough to pass a multiple-choice exam, but such knowledge does not constitute wisdom. The deeper we understand the evil wrought by Hitler or Stalin, the more we know to respect the capacity for evil that lurks in every heart. If we are intellectually and morally lazy and look back at Hitler or Stalin from the safe remove of historical distance, we risk falling into the trap of tautology: Hitler was evil because he was evil. Stalin killed millions because he was a killer.

There was much more to it than that. If we are to learn lessons from the dark chapters of history, we must understand them in detail. We must view them as timeless indictments that must constantly be summoned in the here and now to keep us alert and vigilant; those who take the opposite view, that the infinite infamy of a Hitler or Stalin rules out ever comparing their strategies or tactics to the strategies and tactics of our contemporaries, might as well start burning books, the way Hitler himself did. Just as we must look at great Presidents and other leaders to see how and why they did what they did, we must also be alert to the negative example of when power has been obscenely misused. I caused quite a commotion in early 2005 when I spoke out against a Republican scheme to bypass the rules of Congress. Their goal was to subvert the will of the Framers of the Constitution, and I openly defied them.

"Many times in our history we have taken up arms to protect a minority against the tyrannical majority in other lands," I said on the Senate floor on March 1, 2005.

We, unlike Nazi Germany or Mussolini's Italy, have never stopped being a nation of laws, not of men. But witness how men with motives and a majority can manipulate law to cruel and unjust ends. Historian Alan Bullock writes that Hitler's dictatorship rested on the constitutional foundation of a single law, the Enabling Law. Hitler needed a two-thirds vote to pass that law, and he cajoled his opposition in the Reichstag to support it. Bullock writes that "Hitler was prepared to promise anything to get his bill through, with the appearances of legality preserved intact." And he succeeded.

"Hitler's originality lay in his realization that effective revolutions, in modern conditions, are carried out with, and not against, the power of the state: the correct order of events was first to secure access to that power and then begin his revolution. Hitler never abandoned the cloak of legality; he recognized the enormous psychological value of having the law on his side. Instead, he turned the law inside out and made illegality legal."

I would have thought anyone who had ever learned the lessons of the Founding Fathers would recognize in my words their insistence on providing the architecture for a republic that would be based always on the rule of law, even when ruthless politicians in the executive branch tried to short-circuit the Founders' intent. If we go halfway in our commitment to the rule of law, it is a slippery slope toward runaway unaccountability and abuse of power. It is pointless to argue about whether our institutions are strong enough to protect us from ever producing an infamous monster to compare with a Hitler and Stalin. We can only hope so. And we can only guard against any slippage, any progress down that slippery slope, away from the wisdom of the men who launched our young nation.

I struck a raw nerve by mentioning Hitler in that Senate floor speech. I did not do so rashly. I have not put myself through fifty years of wrangling in the Senate only to back off easily. I thought at the time that the point I was making was right, and I know now that it was right. In public life one sometimes has to speak bluntly and make statements that will earn howls of protest. From the way some of my opponents carried on, it was easy to forget that in 2002 Senator Phil Gramm had objected to a tax plan by declaring, "Now, forgive me, but that is right out of Nazi Germany. I don't understand . . . why all of a sudden we are passing laws that sound as if they are right out of Nazi Germany?"

Rick Santorum of Pennsylvania, who has since been voted out of the Senate, claimed wildly that merely by mentioning Hitler, I was equating Republicans with Nazis. "These comments lessen the credibility of the Senator and the decorum of the Senate," he said. "He should retract his statement and ask for pardon. . . . What the Democrats are doing is the equivalent of Adolf Hitler in 1942 saying, 'I'm in Paris. How dare you invade me. How dare you bomb my city. It's mine.'"

Sometimes I think Senate oratory is a lost art. Cartoonish displays of the sort in which Mr. Santorum specialized may make interesting television, but they lack the ring of truth and therefore the capacity to compel a person to adjust his thinking. If history is a stranger to a leader, that leader will forever be surprised by its lessons. History, like life, has its ugly days. But we cannot avert our gaze from its darker chapters; that is a luxury we can never allow ourselves.

Kurt Vonnegut had a firsthand look at the aftermath of the apocalyptic firebombing of Dresden, Germany, late in World War II and used those searing experiences in his classic novel *Slaughterhouse Five,* with his memorable character Billy Pilgrim, a vivid example of a man who has learned the hard lessons of history. He is unstuck in time, bouncing from year to year, history's plaything, as are we all. "History is merely a list of surprises," Vonnegut wrote. "It can only prepare us to be surprised again."

Study history—not only the history of our own great country, but the history of the Roman Republic from whence many of our constitutional principles were derived. Read *The Federalist Papers.* The Framers' intent becomes much clearer. Encourage our citizens to become familiar with our history and the Constitution. Call upon them to vote regardless of party. We need active citizens who understand and participate in government at every level. We can do better.

4. A BIG LIE IS STILL A LIE: TELL THE TRUTH

We have our strengths, as a country, which I have in this letter delineated, but we also have a glaring weakness: Lies at the top of government can have a deeply corrosive effect on the quality of our democracy for which there are no ready answers. "False words," observed Plato, "are not only evil in themselves, but they infect the soul with evil."

Friedrich Nietzsche presciently identified the manner in which much of the public would react to President George W. Bush's fast and loose way with the truth when he commented, "I'm not upset that you lied to me, I'm upset that from now on I can't believe you."

It is, alas, a slippery slope, in which one lie necessitates another lie and another and another in an age-old cycle. As Sir Walter Scott put it, "Oh what a tangled web we weave / When first we practice to deceive!" A fire wall must be built against the fundamental threat to our democracy posed by the rampant willingness to lie. We who would serve the public must think first and foremost of the trust we must always seek to build with the people, and that trust must be built on truthfulness and directness. Dear new President, do not lie to the public. Set an example of humility and honesty.

I was elected to high office in another era, and have never seen any reason to turn my back on the lessons my coal-miner father instilled in me growing up in Wolf Creek Hollow. We were not fancy people and did not trade in the layers of meaning that fancy people might find fashionable. I have adhered to a simple and unambiguous standard my whole time in elective office: I never—*never*—intend to mislead. I have always intended to be up front.

Sometimes a politician has to be careful with his words. If you slip up with words as you explain a complicated or sensitive situation, you can be in trouble. As Mark Twain said, "The difference between the right word and almost right word is the difference between lightning and a lightning bug." But there is a line between caution and falsehood that everyone feels in their bones, and no matter how convoluted a justification he or she may offer, the person who tells a lie knows he or she is lying.

We cannot shy away from calling a lie a lie. If a President inserts a clear falsehood in his State of the Union address, that is a lie. No other word will do. For some reason which I will likely never be able to fathom, a reluctance has grown to call a lie a lie. That is part of the problem. Since no one wants to call a lie a lie anymore, it becomes less forbidden, less dangerous, every time we shy away from having the courage and honesty to come right out and say, "That's a lie." To quote William Cullen

Bryant, the great poet and journalist for whom Bryant Park in Manhattan was named:

> *Truth, crushed to earth, shall rise again,—*
> *The eternal years of God are hers;*
> *But Error, wounded, writhes in pain,*
> *And dies among his worshippers.*

Our culture has experienced a stark decline in the moral framework that impels anyone of good character to feel a stigma about lying. We have seen a diminution in the common perception that it is immoral to lie. The cycle of justification sets in and all becomes possible. It's a trend all through politics and indeed all through our society. Everybody thinks, Well, it's not so bad, let's just spin it this way or spin it that way and save everybody embarrassment or save everybody from having to admit a mistake.

We cannot continue down this path, new President. We must rebuild a culture of intolerance to lying, and that must start close to home. I have made a practice for many years of sitting down each and every staff member who comes to work for me and drawing a clear line in the sand. "Never mislead people," I tell them. "Do not tell them we can do things we likely cannot do."

Sometimes a politician must disappoint people. "No" is the most important word in politics and one of the hardest to utter. But it is foolhardy to try to be all things to all people. Many a time, a constituent has come to see me and made a request and I have had to look that constituent in the eye, calmly but forcefully, and say, "No, I'd love to help you, but I cannot do what you ask." He may recoil at first. He may be disappointed. But in the end he respects that someone had the honesty and character to speak the truth to him.

That is especially true of how the people react to their leader, which is why the President of the United States must adhere to the highest standards of honesty. I say that to you now, new President, and it is truer than ever, given the severe loss of public faith in the level of truth in White House pronouncements, but I have never been shy about criticizing a President from either party for falling short.

My regard for the achievements of Bill Clinton as President has grown over time. His was, as we know, a flawed presidency, as I will discuss, but it is also true that instead of running for office pledging to be "a uniter, not a divider," and then settling into the White House as the most divisive, most nakedly partisan President in my lifetime, Clinton embarked during his eight years in office on a good-faith effort to bring the country together. The public turned against the activist Republican Congress led by Newt Gingrich and gave Clinton their support because the great middle of the country, the people drawn to neither extreme, saw that the Clinton administration had their interests in mind with a series of programs and with a disciplined budget approach that helped launch a surge in job creation and the longest economic expansion in our history.

I was not shy in speaking up when Bill Clinton disappointed me. As the Monica Lewinsky matter began to turn into a full-fledged scandal, I used whatever influence I had in the Senate to counsel restraint and moderation and appropriate levels of disapprobation. I was also insistent that the questions of truthfulness that had been raised demanded serious attention.

"Many of the mistakes that President Nixon made are being made all over again," I said in September 1998, referring to what looked to me like a cover-up. "We seem to be living history all over again."

But I also warned against a herd mentality.

"If sometime in the future, the American people should come to believe that this President or any other President has been driven out of office for what they may perceive to be political reasons, their wrath will fall on those who jumped to judgment prematurely."

The following January, on the eve of Clinton's impeachment trial in the Senate, I was tough in my criticism. I made clear that I had not yet decided which way I would vote and also issued a sharp criticism of the press conference the President held one day after the House approved two articles of impeachment.

"That was an egregious display of shameless arrogance, the likes of which I don't think I have seen," I said in one television interview.

Describing the confusion at that time, Cokie Roberts of *World News Tonight* reported on January 5, "Part of it is that you have conservative Republicans who just want to torture the

President for as long as they humanly can. But part of it is that you have serious constitutionalists who really think the process should play out, Senator Byrd among them."

Over on the *NBC Nightly News,* correspondent Lisa Myers reported on my position on the controversy as well, calling me "the Senate's most respected voice on impeachment, a Democrat known for integrity and independence." She added: "The Senator's words carry special weight because he's a scholar, has written books on the Senate, and its rules and traditions. Most politicians quote public opinion polls; Byrd quotes the founding fathers and Greek and French philosophers."

Later that month, I released a statement saying I intended to introduce a motion to end the impeachment trial, concluding: "It is necessary that we begin now the process of healing and reconciling the differences caused by these events and address together the issues, challenges and opportunities facing our nation."

In the end I voted no on both counts against President Clinton, and I am glad that I did. But before I came to that conclusion, I agonized long and hard, as I explained that year on the February 7 edition of the Sunday program *This Week* on ABC: "I have to live with myself. I have to live with my conscience. And I have to live with the Constitution."

I beg your pardon, new President, if this review of a deeply painful episode in our nation's history brings you particular pain, but I feel it is important to make the point that one must stand against lies, large and small, whether they come from the lips of Democrats or Republicans. I think my stern judgment of President Clinton was appropriate at the time, but looking back one cannot help but yearn for the standards of truth and honesty extant during the Clinton administration, compared to what the nation has been subjected to in the years since Bill Clinton left office.

The Bush administration, not to put too fine a point on it, built much of its program around a basic commitment to lying. Bush and those around him understood the power of an artful lie to influence and shape perceptions. As Mark Twain observed, "A lie can travel halfway around the world while the truth is still putting on its shoes." Very late in the Bush years, long after the nation had soured on the President and opposed him on a variety of fronts, according to all the polls, Bush and the people around him were still unwilling to give up or scale down their promiscuous twisting of the truth. No lie was too egregious or transparent for the administration to have any qualms about repeating it over and over and over in a cynical attempt to make people start to think it might be true. In this tactic, the administration adopted an approach counseled by the father of the Soviet state, Vladimir Ilyich Lenin, and the führer of the Third Reich, Adolf Hitler.

"A lie told often enough becomes the truth," said Lenin.

"Make the lie big, make it simple, keep saying it, and eventually they will believe it," said Hitler.

FDR, in contrast, asserted, "Repetition does not transform a lie into a truth."

I do not wish to tarry overlong on a catalog of what I see as the more important lies of the Bush administration, but a good place to start would be his run for President. Everyone knew the reason he was running was because his name was George Bush. His father had been Vice President for eight years and President for four. His grandfather, Prescott Bush, had been a United States Senator, and for four years Senator Bush and I served together. The young Bush was a product of Washington privilege. Yes, he had spent some time in Texas, but he was a product of East Coast old money and had gone to a fancy prep school and Yale University, where he was a member of the secret society Skull and Bones. This man never knew what it was to live behind the railroad tracks, to feed the hogs and gather up the scraps and go to school with that on the pants of your overalls.

Yet when George W. Bush ran for President he tried hard to present himself as some kind of common-man outsider. Everyone knew this was false, but he kept repeating the line and the press went along with it. At one point, trying to sell his outsider credentials, he said, "I've never lived in Washington in my life," a clear falsehood, since as *The Washington Post* later reported, he had lived there for eighteen months in 1987 and 1988 with a full-time job playing a role in his father's presidential campaign. It should not be so easy to say "never," in clear violation of the truth, and yet it seemed this President was more comfortable with conviction, based on a leap of faith, than with fidelity to the facts.

The shocking part was the frequency with which he would

literally say one thing and then, a week or a month later, decide on saying the opposite, and then expect the American people to believe him both times. As but one example, and there are too many to count, between December 2003 and August 2006, the Bush strategy in the disastrously botched Iraq War was "to stay the course," as the President himself insisted in public at least six times over that period—on December 15, 2003; April 5, April 13, and April 16, 2004; August 4, 2005; and August 30, 2006.

Then the President appeared on ABC's *This Week* and host George Stephanopoulos, bending over backward to ask an easy question, mentioned that former Secretary of State James Baker, a coleader of the Iraq Study Group, "says that he's looking for something between 'cut and run' and 'stay the course.'"

"Well, hey, listen, we've never been 'stay the course,' George," President Bush declared on national television. "We have been— we will complete the mission, we will do our job, and help achieve the goal, but we're constantly adjusting to tactics. Constantly."

WAR IS PEACE. FREEDOM IS SLAVERY. IGNORANCE IS STRENGTH. It was as if ABC had suddenly cut into *This Week* with the film version of *1984,* starring John Hurt as Winston Smith, and we were suddenly listening to Big Brother adjusting the party line every day, and expecting the cowed masses to go along. Not in America, Mr. Bush.

The nation can and does demand more of its leaders, and you, new President, must do your part to win back trust. It will be harder to regain the confidence of the American people than it was for that confidence to be drowned in a river of falsehoods. I do not think that we as a nation can afford any more of that. It will not always be easy for you to meet challenging circumstances with the truth. But there is inspiration in the Scriptures: "So Jesus said to those Jews who had believed in Him, If you abide in My word, you are truly My disciples. And you will know the Truth, and the Truth will set you free." (John 8:31)

5. BUILD YOUR PRESIDENCY
AROUND ACCOUNTABILITY

H*arry Truman came to West Virginia* in 1958 and I will never forget that visit because of a seemingly small detail. Truman delivered a fiery speech at the Charleston Municipal Auditorium and did a wonderful job of supporting me in my campaign for the United States Senate. What I remember most, though, came after his speech. He had already reached the rear of the auditorium, eager to make his exit and catch a plane for Pittsburgh, when he realized he had forgotten something and came back to look for me.

"Where are those two daughters?" he asked me.

I had mentioned before his speech that both my young daughters, Mona and Marjorie, would very much like his autograph. He promised to grant their wish. Almost out of the door, he came back so he could sign autographs for my two girls, and they were delighted that he had. To me that was a true sign of greatness. Truman was an earthy man and never forgot to treat people right. He was a man who always held himself accountable to his own personal standards. That in my experience is a rare thing in politics.

"No one man can really fill the Presidency," Truman once said, ever the modest man. "[It] is an executive job that is almost fantastic. No absolute monarch has ever had such decisions to make or the responsibilities that the President of the United States has."

Truman had only been Vice President for eighty-three days when he walked into the office of the Speaker of the House, Sam Rayburn, for a visit on April 12, 1945, and was told he had to hurry to the White House "as quickly and as quietly" as he could. Once there, he was sent up to Eleanor Roosevelt's study on the second floor and as he walked in, Mrs. Roosevelt put her arm across his shoulders.

"Harry," she said, "the President is dead."

Truman was stunned into speechlessness and had to fight back tears. Finally he spoke.

"Is there anything I can do for you?" he asked Mrs. Roosevelt.

"Is there anything *we* can do for *you*?" she replied. "For you are the one in trouble now."

Two hours later, Truman stood in the White House Cabinet Room and was sworn into office by Chief Justice Harlan F. Stone. He was in a sense an accidental President, thrust into that awesome responsibility suddenly and abruptly, and from the beginning he was universally underestimated. He stood five feet eight, had a folksy, no-nonsense style, and reminded many people more of a banker or businessman from Independence,

Missouri, than a national leader. He had no college degree. None of that mattered for the simple reason that Truman confronted his responsibilities directly and never took a pass on the hand that history had dealt him. He was comfortable with himself and had a disarming way of showing it.

"Boys, if you ever pray, pray for me now," he told reporters in the first days of his presidency. "I've got the most terribly responsible job a man ever had."

Truman was also tough-minded enough to make some of the most difficult choices any President has ever made. He led the nation through some of its most momentous days—making the decision to drop the atomic bombs on Hiroshima and Nagasaki; averting the complete loss of Europe to the Soviet Union with his calm decisiveness during the crisis that spawned the Berlin Airlift starting in 1948; putting in motion the Marshall Plan and establishing the North Atlantic Treaty Organization, which together would transform postwar Europe; and ordering U.S. troops into Korea to guard against communist expansion.

But as much as anything, Truman will always be remembered for the "Give 'em hell, Harry" fighting spirit that he showed in the 1948 campaign, and for his insistence on taking personal responsibility for the actions and policies of his administration. Truman's friend Fred Canfil, a U.S. marshall in Missouri, visited the Federal Reformatory in El Reno, Oklahoma, and had a thirteen-inch-long sign made for the President, mounted on a walnut base. On one side it said THE BUCK STOPS HERE!—a takeoff on the expression "passing the buck," which was never Truman's way—and on the other I'M FROM MISSOURI! The sign was mailed to Truman in October 1945 and soon became part of his legacy.

"The greatest part of the President's job is to make decisions . . . ," Truman said in his farewell address when he left the White House in January 1953. "The papers may circulate around the government for a while, but they finally reach this desk. And then, there's no place else for them to go. The President— whoever he is—has to decide. He can't pass the buck to anybody. No one else can do the deciding for him. That's his job."

Two years later, speaking in French Lick, Indiana, he said, "When I was at the White House I used to keep on my desk a sign which said, 'The Buck Stops Here!' That is a precept every President ought to have on his desk. And, what is more, he ought to meet it."

I could not agree more, new President. It is vital to have the man or woman in charge say: Hold me accountable! We have lived through years in which running from accountability was the new national sport, especially at the White House. No one was accountable. It was always, "What happened?" or "How did that happen?" or "How did that get into my speech? Was it Condoleezza Rice?" If a President can never admit to having made a single mistake in office, perhaps we ought not to have been shocked that he worked to avoid accountability at every turn, both for himself and for anyone who worked for him.

This must not continue. Please, new President, do not brook incompetence or corruption in your administration. No one is indispensable, including yourself. Do not be hesitant to fire miscreants or fools in your cabinet. You owe the American people competent, honest stewards of their money and their lives. Accountability has long been missing in politics. See that it returns in your administration. Only through accountability to the people can we ensure that democracy will continue to thrive, as James Madison explored in "Federalist No. 49."

As the people are the only legitimate fountain of power, and it is from them that the constitutional charter, under which the several branches of government hold their power, is derived, it seems strictly consonant to the republican theory, to recur to the same original authority, not only whenever it may be necessary to enlarge, diminish, or new-model the powers of the government, but also whenever any one of the departments may commit encroachments on the chartered authorities of the others [he wrote]. The several departments being perfectly co-ordinate by the terms of their common commission, none of them, it is evident, can pretend to an exclusive or superior right of settling the boundaries between their respective powers; and how are the encroachments of the stronger to be prevented, or the wrongs of the weaker to be redressed, without an appeal to the people themselves, who, as the grantors of the commissions, can alone declare its true meaning, and enforce its observance?

The example of Harry Truman, once dismissed as an accidental President, now held aloft as a paragon of presidential greatness by Democrats and Republicans alike, illustrates the positive impact of establishing accountability as a founding principle of your administration, new President. To look at a negative example of what happens when accountability is nowhere to be found, let us turn back to one of the more bizarre chapters in U.S. history, a strange and twisted saga involving among other things a cake shaped like a key, brought by the president's representatives to Iran to present to the Ayatollah Khomeini along with a Bible personally signed by the President. I am referring, of course, to the Iran-contra scandal that unfolded during the administration of Ronald Reagan, a scandal that amounted to a direct and flagrant flouting of the Constitution.

The scandal was in direct conflict with steps taken by Congress in the aftermath of the Vietnam War to place limits on the unchecked power of the presidency. Congress passed legislation in the early 1980s specifically designed to bar U.S. assistance to the CIA-backed contra army waging guerrilla war against the democratically elected government of Nicaragua, a small Central American nation then led by the openly socialist Sandinista party. The Boland Amendment, as it was called, barred the CIA or Defense Department from using funds "to furnish military equipment, military training or advice, or other support for military activities, to any group or individual, not part of a country's armed forces, for the purpose of overthrowing the Government of Nicaragua."

There was, in that language, no room for misunderstanding, and yet the Reagan administration was willing to undermine the

Constitution of the United States, which guarantees the sanctity of law, in order to pursue its harebrained scheme to attempt to overthrow the Sandinistas and back the mercenary army called the contras, which to his lasting shame Reagan had dubbed "the moral equivalent of the Founding Fathers." How could a President know so little about our Founding Fathers? I shudder still at the slander of the great men who made us what we are as a country.

Reagan was not shy about speaking in public of Iran as the most heinous of outlaw states, saying at one point that it was "run by the strangest collection of misfits, Looney Tunes and squalid criminals since the advent of the Third Reich." Yet in order to secure the release of hostages held in Lebanon by groups aligned with Iran, Reagan's National Security Council staff cooked up the scheme to offer Iran ransom to free the hostages—and for that ransom delivered weapons to our enemies, using the money from those arms sales to fund the contra mercenaries.

When the scandalous scheme became public in November 1986, Reagan denied it: "In spite of the wildly speculative and false stories about arms for hostages, we did not, repeat, did not trade arms or anything else for hostages," he insisted.

That story unraveled in no time. Reagan had to admit the truth within four months, telling the nation, of his earlier denial, "My heart and my best intentions still tell me that is true, but the facts and the evidence tell me it is not."

That was not, however, what was told to me when I visited the White House on November 12, soon after the revelations became news, in my role as Senate Minority Leader, along with Senate

Majority Leader Bob Dole, House Majority Leader Jim Wright, and none other than Dick Cheney, then a congressman, there in his role as assistant minority leader. We wanted answers from the President and the other high-ranking administration figures in the meeting, including Vice President George H. W. Bush, Secretary of State George Shultz, Attorney General Edwin Meese, Admiral John Poindexter, the national security adviser, and Chief of Staff Donald Regan. In particular we wanted to know why a President who had repeatedly vowed that he would not make any secret deals to secure the release of hostages had done just that, and Reagan for the first time personally acknowledged that his administration had funneled military equipment to our enemies in Iran.

As Donald Regan's notes of the meeting later revealed, even at that late date Admiral Poindexter gave us a false story, insisting that "Israel's participation in arms selling led us to discover arms in Portugal which Israel [was] selling to get Jews out of Iran."

I was skeptical, and pushed for clear information as to when the Reagan administration had begun its private dealings with Iran. Poindexter again resorted to falsehood, insisting that "no transfer of material" had occurred before a Presidential finding was signed in January 1986 to attempt to provide legal cover.

The blatant dishonesty and shifting rationales fueled widespread outrage and turned the Iran-contra scandal, as it was soon known, into a national fixation, complete with televised hearings. This was, above all, a story about the importance for any U.S. President of being accountable—to the Congress, yes, but most of all to the American people and to the Constitution. Sadly, that lesson was lost on Reagan and his aides, especially his Vice President, the elder George Bush.

Let us fast-forward a few years to the tail end of the first Bush's one term as President. Shultz, Reagan's Secretary of State, would later publish a book in 1993 in which he emphasized that Vice President Bush was in the loop on the arms-for-hostages deal, and that Shultz was later "astonished" to hear Bush denying that he knew about the deal, when he obviously knew all about it.

As *The New York Times* reported, "In one instance, Mr. Shultz says, he complained to Nicholas F. Brady, then a Bush aide, that the Vice President had said on television that it was inconceivable to even consider selling arms to Iran when hostages were being held by pro-Iranian extremists in Lebanon. 'The Vice President was in one key meeting that I know of, on Jan. 7, 1986, and he made no objection to the proposal for arms sales to Iran, with the clear objective of getting hostages released in the process,' Mr. Shultz quotes himself as telling Mr. Brady on Nov. 8, 1986. . . .' "

Bush and Shultz met for drinks and the Vice President "admonished" the Secretary of State, "asking emphatically whether I realized that there were major strategic objectives being pursued with Iran. He said he was very careful about what he said."

Shultz said the first George Bush was clearly not being truthful when he told *The Washington Post* in August 1987, "If I had sat there and heard George Shultz and Cap express it [opposition to the scheme] strongly, maybe I would have had a stronger view. But when you don't know something, it's hard to react. We were not in the loop."

Not in the loop? Does that sound familiar?

Judge Lawrence Walsh's investigation of the shocking scandal was still under way when the first Bush issued a dramatic series of six pardons on Christmas Eve 1992, just weeks before Bill Clinton was inaugurated, apparently hoping to attract little attention with the holiday season as cover. I would have thought our celebration of Christ's birthday might be honored more assiduously than that, but never mind.

The pardons of Caspar Weinberger and five others involved in the Iran-contra scandal were clearly designed to halt Judge Walsh's investigation before it directly implicated George H. W. Bush himself, and sadly, they succeeded. Walsh was so outraged, he said, "The Iran-contra cover-up, which has continued for more than six years, has now been completed." The pardons had nullified three guilty pleas and one conviction and put a stop to two pending cases.

Yet to this day, when the press refers to controversial presidential pardons, it invariably gives more attention to Clinton's later pardon of Marc Rich, by all accounts a major mistake and one I characterized at the time as "malodorous." I am in no way opposed to the Rich pardon continuing to invite criticism of President Clinton, yet as a nation, there was little to learn from that episode and much to glean from the Bush 43 Christmas Eve pardons, which derailed an ongoing investigation that could have rewritten the first President Bush's place in history.

We should have learned valuable lessons on accountability from the Iran-contra scandal and the brazen abuse of power with which the first President Bush stifled open inquiry. Instead, we seem to have learned very little. At one time it looked as if the scandal might force President Reagan from high office, and that might have been what would have been necessary to ensure that others would not attempt in the future to try to circumvent the Constitution as Reagan and his key aides clearly did. Instead, the bizarre aspects of the case and its confusing nature ensured that to this day, many of its details remain shrouded in secrecy. We needed to confront this as just the sort of challenge to our democratic traditions that the Founding Fathers had envisioned, but we lacked the attention span for that.

"[T]he plurality of the Executive," Alexander Hamilton wrote in "Federalist No. 70," "tends to deprive the people of the two greatest securities they can have for the faithful exercise of any delegated power, *first,* the restraints of public opinion, which lose their efficacy, as well on account of the division of the censure attendant on bad measures among a number, as on account of the uncertainty on whom it ought to fall; and, *secondly,* the opportunity of discovering with facility and clearness the misconduct of the persons they trust, in order either to their removal from office or to their actual punishment in cases which admit of it."

We knew what we did *not* want, in short, as Hamilton went on to explain: "In England, the king is a perpetual magistrate; and it is a maxim which has obtained for the sake of the public peace, that he is unaccountable for his administration, and his person sacred."

These are episodes in our history of which the people need to be told and told and told; we need to have a national dialogue about the need for accountability. No such dialogue can have meaning unless you, new President, demand of yourself a standard of accountability that would make Harry Truman proud.

6. LET THE PRESS DO ITS JOB, EVEN WHEN THAT MIGHT STING

The national press has evolved dramatically over the years compared to the reporters I remember in Washington in the period following World War II, when change swept over the once-quiet town at so brisk a pace. As former ABC newsman David Brinkley, a beloved presence on Sunday morning television for many a year, wrote in *Washington Goes to War*, describing the late 1940s, shortly before I arrived as a young congressman, it was a "town full of magnolias and mosquitoes, and suddenly it became the capital of the world."

But those reporters in the postwar years at least minded when they were told lies. Those reporters minded when they were treated as fools. If you tried again and again to out-and-out mislead them, and they figured out what you were up to, they would find a way to make you wish you had never dared take that risk. Most of those reporters, I fear, would not recognize what the press has now become. They would be shocked to see how thoroughly a herd instinct kicked in during the pivotal weeks leading up to the Iraq War. Reporters let themselves be stampeded, pure and simple.

The tug-of-war between the press and elected officials goes back deep into our history, all the way back to the Founding Fathers and even before that, if you keep in mind the antecedents of our democratic system of government and consider the colorful history of the institution of the press in England. It goes without saying that one must expect an adversarial edge and the occasional crude tactic on either side of the divide. What we have seen in recent years, however, is something altogether different. If this were a tug-of-war, the rope has broken.

Daniel Okrent, the first ombudsman—or quasi-internal watchdog—ever hired by *The New York Times*, wrote a devastating column on May 30, 2004, doing for the *Times* what every institution responsible for the national breakdown that preceded the Iraq War must do: focus on pointed self-criticism.

"To anyone who read the paper between September 2002 and June 2003, the impression that Saddam Hussein possessed, or was acquiring, a frightening arsenal of W.M.D. seemed unmistakable," Okrent wrote. "Except, of course, it appears to have been mistaken. . . . War requires an extra standard of care, not a lesser one. . . . In 1920, Walter Lippmann and Charles Merz wrote that *The Times* had missed the real story of the Bolshevik Revolution because its writers and editors 'were nervously excited by exciting events.' That could have been said about *The Times* and the war in Iraq."

The problem with the coverage in that period was not only the tone of so much of what was plastered on the front pages of the papers, but also the glaring shortage of sharp and pointed skepticism. This was a deeply disturbing sign of decrepitude in the heart of one of the most essential institutions in our republic. I cannot begin to untangle all the trends and shifts that account for the decline in skepticism in the press, but I can remark upon the swift pace of this change and on its symbolic face: Sam Donaldson, White House correspondent for *ABC News* from 1977 to 1989, and again briefly during the Clinton administration.

Many in Washington will never forget the sight of President Reagan on the White House lawn, hurrying to or away from his helicopter, *Marine One,* and cupping his hand to his ear to catch the shouted questions from the press corps. Donaldson, with his foghorn voice, was the designated shouter much of the time, and became so famous for his earsplitting questions that Reagan used the newsman as the punch line for a joke in 1988 before the annual White House News Photographers' Association. The President was showing slides from his time in office, including one of him on a trip in Indonesia, wearing a most un-Reagan-like garment, a wildly garish shirt with the presidential seal crisscrossed in a pattern probably popular with 1960s counter-culture types. The picture shows the President working to contain a grimace as he looks down at the shirt, which had been presented to him by his Indonesian hosts.

"Actually, I love this shirt," Reagan deadpanned to the White House photographers. "I finally found something louder than Sam Donaldson."

Reagan often joked about Donaldson during his time in the White House, cracking at one point that he saw no need to try to pressure *ABC News* to hit the mute button on Donaldson's questions. "We can't," Reagan said. "If we did, the starlings would come back."

Reagan later said Donaldson's abrasive voice was one thing he would not miss about life in the White House, but at least Reagan often attempted to give some kind of answer. Donaldson, still an occasional guest on the ABC Sunday talk program *This Week,* showed up at a news conference in August 2006 and shouted out a question to President Bush.

"You're a has-been!" Bush answered crudely, shouting right back. "We don't have to answer has-beens' questions!"

A few minutes later, Bush added: "My best moment in here is when my press conference ended."

That, sadly, has been the attitude toward that central pillar of democracy, the public's right to know. It sounds almost quaint to point it out now, but for most of the history of the presidential news conference, the questions were not screened ahead of time, the way they were for George W. Bush. This President knew what questions were coming, and had a neatly arranged list that told him exactly which reporter to call on at exactly which point in the press conference. Bush even joked about it at times, as if there were anything funny about gaming the system and cheating the people of their basic right to have an accountable President. Reporters of an earlier generation would never have stood for that. There was a deep-seated respect among the people of the press. But under Bush it was accepted as a given, and if reporters tried to buck the new rules and ask a question other than what was expected, then they would not be asked back.

Every President from John F. Kennedy to George W. Bush was familiar with Helen Thomas, a longtime reporter for United Press International who for years asked the first question at every presidential press conference. Every President from John F. Kennedy to Bill Clinton afforded Thomas a measure of respect commensurate with her years of experience and undeniable insights into the ways of Washington. Then in early 2003 Thomas gave a talk before the annual banquet of the Society of Professional Journalists and was approached afterward by a young journalist from the *Daily Breeze* in Torrance, California. He asked why she looked sad.

"I should be," Thomas said. "I'm covering the worst President in American history."

Two months later, as an Ann McFeatters article in *Ms.* magazine later explained, Thomas was not called on during a presidential news conference, an obvious and intentional snub that was occurring "for the first time in what reporters believe was more than four decades." Thomas wrote the President to apologize, insisting she did not mean to call him the nation's worst President, and he wrote back to accept. But it wasn't until three years later that she received absolution.

"At the March 21 [2006] press conference . . . Bush then signaled that he was ready, finally, to take a question from the veteran reporter."

This was how the exchange played out.

"You're going to be sorry!" Thomas said.

"Well, then, let me take it back," Bush said.

Thomas continued with her question, a skeptical one about the war in Iraq.

"I'd like to ask you, Mr. President—your decision to invade Iraq has caused the deaths of thousands of Americans and Iraqis, wounds of Americans and Iraqis for a lifetime," Thomas had the temerity to ask. "Every reason given, publicly at least, has turned out not to be true."

There was almost a gasp in the room, since the question was shaping up as such a departure from the typical softballs lobbed in this president's direction.

"My question is: Why did you really want to go to war? . . ." Thomas continued. "You have said it wasn't oil, the quest for oil. It hasn't been Israel or anything else. What was it?"

It was, for far too many of the reporters gathered around Thomas in the briefing room, an embarrassing question. It was clear that at least some of her colleagues wished she would simply disappear. And what of the question? Was it unfair? Was it something that a President should not be expected to answer?

Far from it, as we all understand now. Thousands more lives were lost in Iraq after that presidential news conference, and still the nation never got a straight answer to the question *Why?*

Instead, the President and the administration hopped from explanation to explanation to explanation, lumbering along as gracefully and purposefully as if they were running the three-legged race at a Sunday picnic. The just-departed administration was the least accountable in my lifetime, perhaps in the lifetime of our republic, and President Bush made clear on national television that he felt accountability, in the form of that Helen Thomas question, was beneath him.

"I think your premise, in all due respect to your question and to you as a lifelong journalist—that I didn't want war," Bush fumbled. "To assume I wanted war is just flat wrong, Helen, in all due respect. . . . No President wants war. Everything you may have heard is that, but it's just simply not true."

At least Bush looked awkward as he delivered this patent lie. By the time of that question, it was hauntingly obvious to the American people that this was a war of choice. It was a war that happened only because Bush wanted it, wanted it badly, wanted it desperately, wanted it so much that he was willing to run preposterously huge risks—risks not only for his own standing in history and with the American public, but of course, risks for the fate of the nation and the fate of the world.

So what did Bush do next? In lieu of an honest answer, or a real answer, he resorted to his favorite diversion any time a tough question was ever asked of him through most of his presidency. That's right, Bush saw that it was time to wave his magic wand and conjure the words that could quiet any challenge to his absolute authority. All he needed to do was spout the code, recite the magic digits—9 and 11—and he was back in never-never land, free to spin whatever fantasies happened to come to mind.

"My attitude about the defense of this country changed on September the 11th," the President said, as his answer to Thomas' question of "Why?" "When we got attacked, I vowed then and there to use every asset at my disposal to protect the American people. Our foreign policy changed on that day, Helen."

Walter Lippmann, one of our first great newspaper columnists, wrote his "Today and Tomorrow" column for thirty-six years, twice winning the Pulitzer prize, and for him the influence that came with appearing in two hundred newspapers brought with it responsibility. He saw it as his duty to remain ever intellectually serious but without sacrificing a bedrock of humility. Lippmann was withering in his judgment of political commentators who fall into the trap of self-importance.

Each of us, I suppose, experiences at some time the nausea of ideas [Lippmann observed in an August 1915 book review]. The language of thought goes stale in us, the fabric of theories and impression seems overworn and musty. . . . That is what kills political writing, this absurd pretense that you are delivering a great utterance. You never do. You are just a puzzled man making notes about what you think. You are not building the Pantheon, then why act like a graven image? You are drawing sketches in the sand which the sea will wash away. . . . The truth is you're afraid to be wrong. And so you put on these airs and use these established phrases, knowing that they will sound familiar and will be respected. But this fear of being wrong is a disease. You cover and qualify and elucidate, you speak vaguely, you mumble because you are afraid of the sound of your own voice. And then you apologize for your timidity by frowning learnedly on anyone who honestly regards thought as an adventure, who strikes ahead and takes his chances.

Harry Truman well understood the need for an active and involved press. "A President who fails to communicate with the people forthrightly and courageously runs the risk of fostering a public detachment or, what could be even worse, a loss of public confidence," he said in the late 1960s. "Presidents from the time of George Washington have been subjected to attacks and abuse. It is a way that a free and open society keeps its government institutions on the alert. It is a small price to pay for an aroused and active public opinion."

I freely admit to being somewhat in the dark when it comes to sorting out the ever greater emphasis people in politics have placed on misleading the press. I always found honesty and directness to be the best policy in dealing with reporters. That is what the people of West Virginia expect of me, and I would hate to disappoint them. The press represents the voice of the people. The press is the eyes and ears of the voters. My first rule in dealing with the press has always been the same as my first rule in dealing with most everyone: *Don't say too much. Say very little.*

Or in other words, don't speak unless you have something to say and don't try to get too clever or fall in love with the sound of your own voice.

As Senate Majority Leader from 1977 to 1981, I was expected to reach out to the press and I had my own way of doing that. Every Saturday, I would call together a small group of ten to fifteen reporters for the kind of talk that might actually lead to everyone in the room leaving with a greater understanding of the issues. I never believed in pampering anyone, including reporters. We served up some coffee, but that was it. They were there to ask me pointed questions and to hear my honest thoughts. Now it seems that no one has time for that kind of exchange anymore.

I always tried to be dignified. I wasn't one of these backslapping, laughing kinds of guys. This was serious business. I was never shy about telling a reporter if I did not think much of a question. That did not happen often, though. The reporters who came to those sessions tended to be very well informed. They did not vault into journalism from exclusive schools, for the most part; usually they worked their way up, which meant a lot of time spent doing their homework and gaining a deep knowledge of Washington and, in particular, the United States Senate. Reporters in those days actually understood Senate procedure. They had read the bills under discussion and knew just what was in them and what was not. But they were always looking to learn more, and I think that is why so many reporters at that time seemed to enjoy those Saturday morning sessions.

I understand that nowadays reporters would never sit still for that kind of probing session, especially not every Saturday. The rules of the game have changed. Pursuing information is not seen as being as central to the job as it was for reporters twenty years ago. They would probably deny that, of course, but the advent of something called the twenty-four-hour news cycle has without doubt shifted the demands of the job. It used to be that reporters had one deadline a day, whether it was five o'clock or seven o'clock in the evening, and that schedule gave them more time to get up to speed on a development and really digest the material. They talked to people and consulted documents and ferreted out the information on their own. It was not possible to become an instant expert, the way it is now. Quick online searches were of course unheard of then. So people with deep knowledge on a subject, whether Senators or journalists, were held in high esteem.

If we had a Walter Lippmann on the scene in recent years, he would be someone on the order of a Thomas L. Friedman of *The New York Times,* the longtime columnist and distinguished former *Times* foreign correspondent. Many people know Friedman's work through his bestselling books, such as *The World Is Flat: A Brief History of the Twenty-first Century.* As a respected columnist, Friedman was in a unique position to question the rationale for war. He did do that—and yet still emerged as a cheerleader for the war, even directly stating that he had "no problem with a war for oil," so long as it achieved certain objectives.

"Is the war that the Bush team is preparing to launch in Iraq really a war for oil?" Friedman wrote in a January 5, 2003, column. "My short answer is yes. . . . But wait a minute. There is nothing illegitimate or immoral about the U.S. being concerned that an evil, megalomaniacal dictator might acquire excessive influence over the natural resource that powers the world's industrial base."

Compare that with what Friedman wrote on September 30, 2007, under the headline 9/11 IS OVER. This was a passionate cri de coeur, a long-awaited, long-overdue moment of accountability; Friedman was finally confronting directly the sad, sad truth that, for all his fitful and misplaced optimism about the potential for success in Iraq, the war and the rationale for war had taken a tragic toll. We as a nation, he seemed suddenly to be realizing, were badly off track.

"9/11 has made us stupid," Friedman wrote. "I honor, and weep for, all those murdered on that day. But our reaction to 9/11—mine included—has knocked America completely out of balance . . . Before 9/11, the world thought America's slogan was: 'Where anything is possible for anybody.' But that is not our global brand anymore. Our government has been exporting fear, not hope: 'Give me your tired, your poor and your fingerprints.' . . . We can't afford to keep being this stupid! We have got to get our groove back. We need a President who will unite us around a common purpose, not a common enemy."

This is the power of democracy: It has always been, at least in the American experience, a self-correcting system, and I profoundly hope that will prove to be the case once again, dear President. The vitally important lesson here is that as a President, you need these institutions to function. You need to suffer the slings and arrows, and emerge stronger and more sure of yourself, because that is the path to a successful presidency, which does not short-circuit democracy and does not make a habit of bad-faith evasions and mendacity.

A President cannot avoid the reality that a premium must inevitably be placed on presenting a positive interpretation of events. Everyone hops, skips, and jumps to the demands of the twenty-four-hour news cycle, as if the nature of time, rather than our relationship to it, had changed. The essential responsibility of every elected official to his or her constituents remains, however, and it must always be considered a daily necessity to be accountable and answerable to the public that gives him or her legitimacy. A President, any President, may come to resent the power of the press. I would suggest to you, new President, that a healthy and probing press corps is vital to your success or failure in leading the country.

7. WE CAN DO BETTER THAN PHOTO-OP DIPLOMACY

Three months after the trial of Nazi war criminal Adolf Eichmann began in Jerusalem in April 1961, a Yale University researcher named Stanley Milgram began an experiment that would later become famous. Subjects in the Milgram experiments were instructed to push a button they believed would inflict an electric shock on what they thought was another volunteer, seated out of view; even when pushing the button led to screams and complaints about a heart condition from the apparent other volunteer, most test subjects continued. If the subject expressed reservations about seemingly inflicting so much pain, they were told, "The experiment requires that you continue."

In the end, more than 60 percent advanced to apparently inflicting the maximum level of shock, a full 450-volt jolt. People all over the world were amazed to hear the results of the Milgram experiments. To many, they pointed disturbingly to an innate human inability to stand up for what is right. The experiments provided a bracing reminder at the time that, as unique as the crimes of the Third Reich were, it is always well to remember the deep attachment in human nature to obedience.

"Obedience is the psychological mechanism that links individual action to political purpose," Milgram wrote in his subsequent study, *Obedience to Authority: An Experimental View.* "It is the dispositional cement that binds men to systems of authority. Facts of recent history and observation in daily life suggest that for many people obedience may be a deeply ingrained behavior tendency, indeed, a prepotent impulse over-riding training in ethics, sympathy and moral conduct. . . . Conservative philosophers argue that the very fabric of society is threatened by disobedience, and even when the act prescribed by an authority is an evil one, it is better to carry out the act than to wrench at the structure of authority."

The Milgram experiments might help us to understand one of the more disturbing facts about the situation in this country at the time the Iraq War began. According to a *Washington Post* poll conducted in September 2003, fully 69 percent of the American public believed that Saddam Hussein was probably responsible for September 11, even after the war was under way. More than two-thirds! This statistic is a national scandal. It shows the dangers of keeping the public distracted, playing on their rampant apathy, if so many people can jump to a conclusion unsupported by facts. I wonder what percentage of the public would have said they believed the moon was probably made of green cheese if Bush and Cheney and Rice made loud pronouncements alluding to growing lunar cheese content—and added that national security in a post-9/11 world demanded that one take their word for it.

We need to take a step back and look at this. Mark Twain, that great American writer with a knack for cutting to the bone, said it best: "Patriotism is supporting your country all the time, and your government when it deserves it." That goes for the press and administration critics, too. Even when poll after poll was showing system failure—complete system failure, as reflected in that 69 percent finding—far too many people were willing to take the complacent route and pretend it was not deeply alarming that they had been given so false a view of the world during the critical run-up to a war that would claim many thousands of lives.

Some tried to suggest it was understandable if people covered their eyes and leaped blindly, jumping to conclusions about Saddam on the flimsiest of pretexts. "It's very easy to picture Saddam as a demon," John Mueller, a political scientist at Ohio State University, told *The Washington Post*. "You get a general fuzz going around: People know they don't like al Qaeda, they are horrified by September 11th, they know this guy is a bad guy, and it's not hard to put those things together." The suggestion seemed to be that the administration had not been actively working to manipulate the press on this vital point—and by extension that the press had not fallen down on the job and failed in its role as the eyes and ears of the people.

Wesley Clark, the former Democratic presidential candidate and onetime NATO commander, appeared on the NBC program

Meet the Press on June 15, 2003, and gave the lie to that suggestion. It was clear, he said, that "a concerted effort . . . to pin
9/11" on Saddam Hussein began as early as late 2001 and that "it
came from people around the White House." To quote Emerson
again: "People only see what they are prepared to see."

Context is the enemy of gullibility. The more that people
know about a subject, the more that they have mulled it over
and weighed different ideas, the more comfortable they will feel
in coming to their own conclusions. It follows that the less detail
and depth of knowledge one has on a subject, the more easily
one can be manipulated. I am not suggesting that we strive to
become a nation of Ph.D.s, nor do I necessarily think that that
would be a good thing. But there are certain desirable degrees of
engagement that should be obtainable. If more than two-thirds
of the people, for whatever reason, confessed before the Iraq
War that they thought Saddam was responsible for September
11, that is proof positive that they can be persuaded of just
about anything, because of apathy and lack of interest. To put it
another way, many of our citizens have become like ships un-
moored. They have abandoned their anchors, if indeed they
were ever truly anchored, and now drift with the tides. Take my
word for it, please, it was not ever thus. Increasingly, the prevail-
ing attitude is one of "Just go with the flow, wherever that might
take us."

New President, you must lead a spirited and unflagging effort
to bring a new excitement and energy to the political culture in
Washington in order to free the people from this dispirited

drift. My belief in the good of the average American has never changed, but these are dangerous currents and must be identified as such. A sharper and clearer discussion with the public on the issues of the day must become the ordinary instead of the extraordinary. Trivia and nonsense cannot be allowed to hold sway.

There is a reason why people the world over think of Hollywood when they think of movies and television programs that they want to see. The American entertainment industry has been the envy of the world for decades because of the simple fact that these people are very good at what they do. They create flashy, dynamic entertainment that grabs people's attention and does not let go. Advertising techniques are almost frighteningly effective.

The typical thirty-second political spot may not always get great reviews, but by and large it is all too effective. Such spots offer little or no information, and seldom if ever challenge a viewer to actually think. The aim is rather to paint an opponent in a ridiculous or negative light, making a potential voter laugh with disdain or grow angry with outrage. Emotion is a much more effective tool for influence than cold, rational thought. Political ad experts are quite adept at zeroing in on the precise emotion they want to trigger.

Even if the recent election cycle that wound up electing you as the forty-fourth President of the United States was in some ways an improvement on the status quo, with its periodic attention to arguments about substantive issues of the day, we are nowhere near to prompting the kind of national dialogue we must have if our system of government is going to thrive. People have to *re*-learn how to think for themselves. Reading critically and challengingly must come back into fashion. Patience and love of learning must be taught instead of speed for speed's sake. Differing views must not only be tolerated, they must be revered.

Change is a constant, and always will be, I expect. People continually rotate in and out of Washington. Bright, young people arrive to work as pages and interns and junior staffers. New Senators and House representatives are elected and others are sent home. New ideas and new approaches to governance are brought forward, now and then, and make an impact or wind up on the ash heap of history. Styles of leadership and fixations of the moment pass with the seasons, inexorably but seldom quietly, and from year to year we bounce back and forth from one familiar set of concerns to another and then, within a few years, back again. It can take some time in Washington to understand just how cyclical much of the underlying dynamic of government turns out to be, and many more years to understand those cycles and to glean at least a limited understanding of when one cycle might be about to end and another to start. This cyclical nature makes me believe that even some of the most dramatic trends, such as the alarming surfeit of superficiality in the way world events are covered in the news, may be poised for a natural correction. I profoundly hope so.

New President, I watched with interest as Bill Clinton's second Secretary of State, Madeleine Albright, embarked on an energetic campaign to go to the media and use face-to-face encounters to involve people of all walks of life in thinking about the U.S. role in international affairs and, more particularly, in building support for certain Albright priorities.

"I thought and still do that one of my prime jobs here is to reconnect the American people with foreign policy and to make it understandable and to make it interesting and to make it meaningful on a very particular basis," Albright said in 1997. "So in terms of what my goals have been, one of my prime goals initially was to create a platform for being able to do the basic foreign policy issues. And that platform included going out to the American public and presenting the case as clearly as possible and relating it to whatever area I was in at the time."

To a certain extent, I was suspicious at first of this effort by Albright. Placing too much emphasis on media campaigns, after all, can be a risky strategy if the attention to media relations does not bring with it a matching commitment to the hard work of policy development and the countless hours of discussions and negotiations, often behind the scenes, on which diplomacy's success or failure normally hinges. However, Albright won many over and did make some progress in helping start a national conversation on crucial issues. I would say, in the end, that she satisfied the need to match presentation with an underlying core of substance. She presented a model of a Secretary of State that the world could see as an involved, passionate advocate for U.S. interests, whose views on the major issues of her time in office were for the most part widely known.

What we saw over the last eight years was a trend toward miniaturization. Watching Colin Powell live on television the fateful day he testified before the United Nations on alleged Iraqi mobile weapons labs and allegedly dangerous aluminum tubes, the sensation was uncanny—almost like seeing General Powell shrink in front of our eyes. As Secretary of State in the Bush administration, Powell was regarded by most Americans as a giant, a man of truly exceptional integrity and accomplishment and, above all, stature. By the time he was unceremoniously dumped by Bush, and even in the years subsequent to his return to private life, Powell looked and sounded more like a mouse: He would let out a squeak now and then, then run back into a hole in the wall and hide from public view. To most people, not only those of us in Washington, it was widely understood that Powell held views highly critical of the Bush administration and of the conduct of the Iraq War. He owed it to his country to speak up. Perhaps one day he finally will.

Historians are unlikely to be kind to Powell's successor, Condoleezza Rice. Every Secretary of State, no matter how formidable his or her brainpower, skill with oratory, or knowledge of geopolitical strategy, can find the job hard going in the absence of maximum access to the President. This was never Rice's problem. She had served briefly in the administration of the first President Bush, though in a fairly junior slot on the National Security Council staff, and had retained warm relations with figures from that administration. She was at Stanford University in California, serving as provost, when she was summoned in 1998

to become the chief foreign-policy tutor to the former president's son, a man who had up to that point demonstrated less
curiosity about the rest of the world than any serious presidential candidate in my lifetime. Nevertheless, Rice tried to make
him sound serious.

"I think that he always had very strong views that allies matter, that you lead your foreign and diplomatic policy from a
point of strength if you start with those who share your values
and share your intentions," Rice claimed in an interview with
Salon.com published in March 2000.

That is, of course, preposterous. Foreign policy cannot be
crafted in such a fashion and true leadership cannot be learned
from a cheat sheet. The Rice teach-a-President leadership school
may have convinced some that Bush could be brought up to
speed to manage superpower relations and other pressing problems of foreign affairs, but Rice's run of success in generating
positive news coverage as Secretary of State brought home the
old adage that manipulation is only manipulation if one does
not enjoy it; if it provides satisfaction, then it gets another
name.

To cite but one example, Rice's credentials as an expert on
international relations were based on her alleged role as an
authority on Russia. The first President Bush introduced her to
Mikhail Gorbachev in December 1989, saying, "This is Condoleezza Rice. She tells me everything I know about the Soviet
Union." If the first Bush, who prided himself on his foreign-
policy knowledge, got everything he knew about the Soviet

Union from Rice, it clearly follows that the younger Bush relied on Rice for his entire approach to Russia. Yet even with a Russia expert in a position of nearly unprecedented access and influence throughout his presidency, George W. Bush took an approach to Russian diplomacy that was nothing short of catastrophic. He made the remark about seeing into Putin's soul after their very first meeting, and then was consistently outmaneuvered through year after year of what some started to call a new Cold War in the waning days of the administration.

As Russian presidential candidate Garry Kasparov, a chess master who formerly ranked number one in the world, joked to comedian Bill Maher in October 2007, "I don't think it makes me feel comfortable just accepting the fact that he outplays your guy."

Kasparov added that Russia under Putin has become a police state with state-controlled media. "I think that with the same tight control of media and the pervasive security force, I believe Bush and Cheney could enjoy the same [high] approval rating here" as Putin enjoys in Russia, according to its state media.

Kasparov criticized the Bush administration for making muddled policy choices in aiding and abetting a movement away from democracy in Russia, all in the name of its plans for Iraq. "When I looked at this administration trying to build democracy in Iraq at the expense of democracy in Russia, I got confused," he said.

"But it went wrong for Bush from the very beginning, because at their first summit Bush tried to play psychiatrist and looked at Putin's eyes searching for his soul, instead of looking at his record," Kasparov said. "Now Putin just is basically spitting in his face by making this open friendship with Ahmadinejad, but it was obvious from the very beginning, because Putin has only one item on his geopolitical agenda: He needs high oil prices and tension in the Middle East helps him to keep the oil prices at an all-time high."

The simple truth is that, for all Rice's success in convincing reporters and even foreign-policy intellectuals of her good credentials, she has consistently chosen style over substance. What one always noticed about Rice's appearances before the cameras, whether she was sitting side by side with an Israeli or Palestinian leader, appearing on the tarmac with a small-country head of state very few Americans could even name, or dragging British Foreign Minister Jack Straw to a football game in her home state of Alabama, the Secretary of State always displayed precisely the same facial expression: a big smile, as if she were having the time of her life and wanted everyone to know it.

I have never been shy about expressing my view that our biographies help establish who we are; my own childhood in Wolf Creek Hollow, among hardworking coal miners and their families, shaped the man I am today. Rice, as a young girl, was a concert pianist, and it seems that the instructions she was given then remain with her today, infusing her every public appearance: Sit with your back straight, and when the time is right, always give them your most dazzling smile, even if you have just gotten your hands crossed and want nothing more than to crawl under the piano.

Sometimes diplomacy must be built on a frown. I was not all smiles when I flew to Yalta to meet with Leonid Brezhnev. What foreign leaders demand of us is not atmospherics or photo ops, but an honest willingness to listen to their concerns. We have given the impression that nothing that happens in the rest of the world is of the slightest value, unless it is done in accordance with U.S. dictates. We should have more influence than any other country in the world, in addition to our muscular power with bombs and bullets. It's time we learn again just how to use that influence so that we may not have to use that power.

8. A NEW APPROACH TO THE REST OF THE WORLD: INFLUENCE

Richard Nixon, a President I respected a great deal for his foreign-policy acumen, wrote in his memoirs that he slept only four hours his first night as the occupant of the White House. That was how oppressed he felt by the weight of his new burdens. Up before 7.00 A.M., he was shaving when his thoughts turned to the secret safe that President Lyndon Johnson had shown him when Nixon visited the White House the previous November.

"When I opened it, the safe looked empty," Nixon wrote. "Then I saw a thin folder on the top shelf. It contained the daily Viet Nam Situation Report for the previous day, Johnson's last day in office. The last page contained the latest casualty figures. I closed the folder and put it back in the safe and left it there until the war was over, a constant reminder of its tragic cost."

Nixon, for all his faults, faced the necessary but daunting lesson that day that every President's tenure is in a vital sense merely an extension of his predecessor's; whatever he or she might do in office exists always within the context of how it builds on—or does

not build on—the work of each and every one of his or her predecessors, and how it might establish a direction that can be carried
on by the long line of future presidents. There is no room, in
short, for knee-jerk emotional decision-making of the sort that
the previous administration made a habit.

I am embarrassed, truly embarrassed, even to mention the extent to which the Bush 43 administration engaged in "ABC
foreign policy"—that is, Anything But Clinton. For example,
whatever the flaws of the Clinton administration's approach to
Kim Jong Il's autocratic and dangerous regime in North Korea,
based strictly on results it was successful. On Clinton's watch,
North Korea's worrisome nuclear-weapons program made exactly no progress, by all accounts, because of a 1994 deal in which
North Korea agreed to freeze its nuclear-weapons program in exchange for U.S. aid and a pledge to pursue direct talks. As a result,
North Korea developed no weapons-grade plutonium in the
Clinton years. U.S. diplomacy was making progress toward a major breakthrough, late in Clinton's final term, but ran out of time.

However, when the new Bush team took over, it put U.S.–North
Korean relations in a deep freeze and killed any momentum toward progress. As if afraid of failure, it started off by refusing to
have anything to do with the Clinton strategy toward North
Korea. This self-defeating approach was all the more stunning
because it stood in direct contrast to the path favored by Bush's
own Secretary of State, Colin Powell, who could not have been
more unequivocal in favoring a continuation of Clinton's work
on this key geopolitical trouble spot.

"As I said previously, and especially in my confirmation hearings, we do plan to engage with North Korea to pick up where President Clinton and his administration left off," Powell said in March 2001. "Some promising elements were left on the table, and we'll be examining those elements."

Powell was absolutely correct: Promising elements had been left on the table. But the good general was in for a rude awakening. As he would learn soon enough, Vice President Cheney and other powerful figures in the administration were dead-set against risking a breakthrough that would in part have been credited to Clinton. Instead, the Bush administration flat-out stalled—letting years go by without making any progress—and resorted to empty name-calling, dubbing North Korea part of an "Axis of Evil" along with Iraq and Iran, and, just as bad, engaged in the politics of personal insult by calling Kim Jong Il, a famously thin-skinned and eccentric individual sensitive enough about his height to wear platform shoes, a "pygmy."

Shortly before the vote in the Senate in October 2002 giving the President authority to wage war against Iraq, the Bush administration found out that North Korea had restarted its nuclear weapons program and "nullified" the 1994 agreement it had reached with the Clinton administration, which was major news indeed. Bush and his top advisers chose to suppress the news and hide this information from the public—and even from the Congress—until after the vote on Iraq, knowing full well that the news of North Korea's aggressive new intentions would have shifted the terms of the debate on war in Iraq. The campaign of public manipulation on Iraq was so omnipresent, it was all but impossible to raise any questions about North Korea, but I nevertheless tried in a Senate floor speech on March 5, 2003.

> While the United States continues its relentless march to war against Iraq, a crisis that is potentially far more perilous is rapidly unfolding halfway around the world on the Korean peninsula, [I said] . . . Mr. President, benign neglect is a dangerous policy to apply to North Korea. The nation is isolated and its people are starving. Kim Jong Il is hostile, erratic, and desperate for cash. He is also armed and heavily fortified. . . . Stalemate and neglect are not effective tools of foreign policy. Wishful thinking is not an effective tool of foreign policy. The situation in North Korea is a crisis, and the United States must come to grips with it. We must open a dialogue with North Korea.

But for reasons I will never grasp, the Bush administration refused to budge and continued its harmful policy of inaction toward North Korea, a policy failure that looked even more incomprehensible in October 2006 when Kim Jong Il tested a nuclear device in a tunnel in northern North Korea, alarming the world. Finally, after years of stalling by claiming it would not negotiate directly with the North Korean regime, the Bush administration reversed course dramatically and agreed to do what I had called for in that Senate speech: practice direct diplomacy, as the Clinton administration before it had. The result was an agreement with North Korea in early 2007, which set up a schedule for North Korea to shut down its recently restarted nuclear program and in return receive fuel-oil shipments from South Korea, as well as a pledge of talks with the U.S. on normalizing relations. To be clear, this was an agreement that could have been arrived at many years earlier if the Bush administration had simply stopped stalling.

The sad saga of recent U.S. relations with North Korea offers a case study in the need for each and every administration to worry first and foremost about getting the job done internationally, not about whether a successful strategy builds on the approach of another administration in a way that might force one President to share credit with one or more predecessors. We really have no choice: Only through a commitment of each administration to avoid working at cross-purposes, wherever possible, can we begin to generate some positive momentum toward change and move forward from the debacle of the Bush years. The stakes are too high for anything less than a coordinated effort that draws together Americans of all political persuasions in a long-term effort to bring to the fore a new international confidence and optimism about U.S. intentions and U.S. actions.

We have all seen the grim polls, new President, but allow me to reflect on them nevertheless. In the last two years of the Clinton presidency, the Pew Global Attitudes Survey found positive opinions of the United States in countries around the world. In fact, only three of the twenty-five countries surveyed did not have at least 50 percent indicating a favorable view of the United States—the three were Pakistan, where only 23 percent had a favorable view, Russia (37 percent), and Nigeria (46 percent). Compare that to 2007, when twenty-two of the forty-six foreign countries surveyed (48 percent) did not have 50 percent or more with a favorable view. That is a truly ominous trend.

Some of the countries where people had held the most favorable views of America saw the most precipitous drops in esteem for us. Poland, for example, checked in with a robust 86 percent of the people holding a favorable view in 1999–2000, but by 2002 the number was down to 79 percent and in 2007 it stood at 61 percent.

What of Britain, our closest ally, led by Tony Blair, whose place in history will forever be haunted by the widespread perception—shared even by his own wife—that he had let himself become a "lap dog" to George W. Bush? Even in Britain, the segment of the population that held a favorable view of the U.S. went from 83 percent in the first survey to 75 percent in 2002 to 70 percent one year later to 58 percent in 2004. We found ourselves truly in trouble in 2007, when only 51 percent of those surveyed in Britain held a favorable view of the U.S.

The bleak trend played out in country after country. In seven years Argentina went from a lukewarm 50 percent favorable to an ice-cold 16 percent, Canada went from 71 percent to 55 percent, and Germany, site of the largest gathering in the world—fully 200,000—to pay respects to the victims of September 11, went from 78 percent holding a favorable view of us in 1999–2000 all the way down to 30 percent in 2007.

We take such numbers lightly only at our own risk. For example, I got a firsthand look at how important the nation of Turkey was and is to U.S. interests back in 1955 on my first trip outside of the United States. During my first term in the House of Representatives, I was lucky to be invited along on an extraordinary journey as a new member of the House Foreign Affairs Committee. Congressman Clement Zablocki headed up our delegation, which climbed aboard a four-engine Constellation and spent more than two months visiting twenty-four countries in the Middle East and Southeast Asia. Even at that time, our study group saw Turkey as a key U.S. ally, and in our report we wrote: "The Turks have given full recognition to the significance of United States aid as an important factor in strengthening Turkey's capacity to stand up against the common enemy (ie, the Soviet Union). To avoid internal unrest Turkey must put more of its slender financial resources into internal developments and a higher standard of living for its people."

That remains a priority for Turkey, which is a key NATO ally with the largest standing army in Europe. It also happens to border Iraq. In the run-up to the Iraq War, the Bush administration made the mistake of taking Turkish cooperation in the war for granted. The Turkish parliament held a vote on allowing U.S. forces into Turkey for the war, which failed by four votes. The bitter and intemperate U.S. reaction to the democratic vote helped put more strain on U.S.-Turkey relations, as did U.S. backing of Iraqi Kurds in Kurdistan. Whatever the explanation, here are the numbers: In 1999–2000, 52 percent of Turks had a favorable view of the U.S. By 2007, only 9 percent of Turks said they had a favorable view of us—the lowest figure for any of the forty-six countries surveyed. For a country as large and important as Turkey to have slipped so far in its attitudes toward the United States counts as a foreign-policy disaster and a slap in the face to the Bush administration.

Understand the art and the value of diplomacy, new President. You will have to invest major energy in restoring America in the eyes of the world. We must banish the image of the disingenuous bully, with one standard for our own behavior and a different one for everyone else's. The President is our Ambassador Supreme and he must restore an image of our country that reflects the character of the American people—tolerant, kind, fair, and willing to use force as a last resort, never a first. Consult often with our allies. We live in a global economy, with a growing international interdependency, and just because the job will be hard and require great patience and diligence does not make it any less necessary.

I believe strongly, new President, that as we move forward as a nation of laws, a nation in which individual liberty is respected both at home and abroad, we will increasingly come to see the years of your predecessor's regime as a tragic detour away from our true path. Many voters of all persuasions had the sense in 2000 that it almost did not matter whether they voted for Al Gore or for George Bush; the country was doing well, our economy was thriving, and even our international role was, after some unsteady first steps early in the Clinton administration, beginning to find a direction. The notion that democratic choice did not matter was, as we all know now, a dangerous illusion.

To be blunt, we have failed as a nation in recent years—we have failed ourselves, first of all, in turning our backs on the Constitution and the basic decency and optimism of our national character, and we have failed the world. But we cannot dwell on that failure, as Henry Ford once wisely counseled. "One who fears the future, who fears failure, limits his activities," he wrote in his autobiography, *My Life and Work*. "Failure is only the opportunity more intelligently to begin again. There is no disgrace in honest failure; there is disgrace in fearing to fail. What is past is useful only as it suggests ways and means for progress."

I believe it useful for us all to take a share of the blame in this failure. I say this as one who took a very public role in opposing the Iraq War and the assault on our basic freedoms and so many other heinous power grabs of recent years. I agree with Mr. Ford's advice that we must use our national failure as a tool to confront our future. That means, when it comes to the U.S. place in the world, not only complaining about the cast of characters who were in lead positions during our great national detour from our true sense of purpose as a country, but also looking as well at the ease with which the demagogues led us astray.

The hard lessons we must learn all point toward the need to expand our sense of our role in the world to include an emphasis not only on our military power, with its power to intimidate and to destroy, as well as to bring chaos and disruption and widespread death, but also on our influence in the world, now at low ebb. That must be restored as quickly as possible, as we all know. I would turn to the words of Samantha Power, formerly the Anna Lindh Professor of Practice of Global Leadership and Public Policy at the John F. Kennedy School of Government and author of the Pulitzer prize–winning study *A Problem from Hell: America and the Age of Genocide.*

> I think that most of us, in a knee-jerk way, tend to conflate power with "hard power"—with economic and military power. [We] would be wise in the 21st century to measure our power by our influence. Influence is best measured not only by military hardware and GDP, but also by other people's perceptions that we, the United States, are using our power legitimately. That belief—that we are acting in the interests of the global commons and in accordance with the rule of law—is what the military would call a "force multiplier." It enhances the U.S. ability to get what it wants from other countries and other players.
>
> The third component of influence—along with traditional hard power and legitimacy—is people's perception that we know what we are doing, that we are competent. Here, one cannot overstate the devastating one-two punch of Iraq and Katrina in undermining the global public's and the American people's faith that the U.S. is a competent prosecutor of its own objectives. . . .

The war in Iraq has thus undermined our hard power by overstretching our military and sending us into deficit. It has undermined our perceived legitimacy because we've ignored the will of the international community and committed grave acts of torture, crimes against humanity, and other terrible sins in the conduct of the war itself. But, crucially, as my [Kennedy school] colleague Steve Walt has put it, we also no longer look like the country that put the man on the moon. Nor does the rest of the world see us, currently, as the country that liberated Europe from two world wars, that devised the Marshall Plan, that helped bring down the Wall. As a result, our ability to get what we want—whether we're talking about ending Iran's nuclear enrichment program, halting genocide in Darfur, reforming the UN, or even securing international buy-in for the effort to stabilize Iraq—our influence has eroded such that we are unable to actually achieve our policy objectives.

So let us speak then of influence, new President, and let us speak of it often. We have a lot of work to do in helping the world to see us the way we can and should be seen. As Thomas Edison said, "Opportunity is missed by most people because it is dressed in overalls and looks like work." We need to embark on an effort to take advantage of the opportunity before us to right our ship of state. We need energetic and freewheeling discussions about our place in the world. That dialogue will not happen on its own. It will require imagination and energy and fresh approaches. The time for campaign slogans has passed.

Now is the time to lead. I ask you to join me and others in working for the following:

TALK TO THE PEOPLE: I think every Congress member and Senator should be asked to make the following pledge: I will spend less time on fund-raising than I will connecting with real voters and bringing them into the national dialogue, both through education and articulation of what I see as important and through careful listening to their concerns and ideas for change. This pledge does not mean having interns answer e-mails. It means "I pledge to spend at least as much of my time back in my district talking to the people, leading town-hall discussions and eating chicken dinners at the Rotary Club or the VFW house or the YMCA, as I will spend on meeting with donors and working with my fund-raising team."

USE OUR AMBASSADORS: It has become commonplace to hear about how the Bush administration has turned anti-Americanism into a worldwide epidemic, and we all know just how richly deserved that ignominious distinction is, based on the numbers I cited earlier. The difficult questions concern what to do next. Many of the admirably animated voices from around the country get carried away in their zest for change. Government of the people can never be the enemy. Our government exists to serve us and to perform duties for all of us, such as maintaining a military and keeping up a nuclear stockpile to serve as a deterrent to full-scale attack. We also need government to use our embassies around the world to bring us closer to our friends and to better understand our enemies. If that sounds quaint, or outmoded, so be it. I think it well worth wondering how we could have gone from being a nation that sent Benjamin Franklin to eighteenth-century Europe as ambassador to France to one that sent Sam Fox to twenty-first-century Europe as ambassador to Belgium.

Franklin needs no introduction, of course. But among his accomplishments, sometimes his years in France are overlooked. Soon after he had helped draft the Declaration of Independence, the Continental Congress sent Franklin to Paris in December 1776 as one of three commissioners. His mission was both vital and almost impossibly difficult, as Stacy Schiff explained in *A Great Improvisation: Franklin, France, and the Birth of America.*

> In the spring of 1776, foreign assistance had been debated as hotly as was independence. The two discussions were inextricably bound; to many the former qualified as the more palatable proposition. The best orator in Congress argued persuasively that a declaration of independence was a necessary step for securing European aid. In that light the document's name constituted a misnomer. It was drafted as an SOS.
>
> "If I call Europe, what number do I call?" Henry Kissinger asked in the 1970s. In the 1770s the answer was obvious. Especially if you had a grievance with Britain, you called Versailles. How you did so was equally obvious, or would become so once others had fumbled along the way. You

summoned the one man in the colonies possessed of that brand of sleek charlatanism known as social grace, the only one of the Founding Fathers familiar with Europe. Few Americans could have risen to Paris's diplomatic or conversational agenda, and even fewer could have done so with the requisite wit, in a language that approximated French. Whether Franklin could succeed in his mission was another question. In the annals of diplomacy his was an original one: Franklin was charged with appealing to a monarchy for assistance in establishing a republic.

Dear President, the fact that you are reading this letter now as a newly elected leader of that republic, more than two centuries later, serves as a testament to Franklin's skill in that mission. As for Sam Fox, the malodorous aspect of his appointment in April 2007 was not merely that he had no apparent qualification for the job of ambassador to Belgium, other than being a major Republican donor. No, the truly disturbing fact about Sam Fox was that he was known, if he was known at all, for having done his best to debase the quality of democracy by having contributed $50,000 to a nonsensically titled group, Swift Boat Veterans for Truth, which traded in lies and misrepresentations in seeking to undermine the 2004 presidential candidacy of my Senate colleague John Kerry. Worse still, the President insisted on sneaking the appointment through as what is called a recess appointment when Congress was out of session. As *The New York Times* noted in an editorial, "It is common for administrations to reward big donors with ambassadorships. But this appointment is a deliberate thumb in the eye of Senator Kerry and fellow Democrats who were poised to reject the nominee."

It was a thumb in the eye of the American people as well, not to mention the people of Belgium. The Sam Fox appointment should serve as a wakeup call to you, new President, and to each of your successors. A balance must be maintained in the men and women we send around the globe to represent U.S. interests. Richard Nixon and Ronald Reagan both pushed the boundaries of what had been considered good taste in appointing friends and cronies to head up our foreign embassies, but both Democrats and Republicans have at times succumbed too often to this temptation. We have too much work to do around the world to miss this opportunity to energize the entire Foreign Service with a new commitment to choosing ambassadors first of all based on merit.

A long tradition exists of political appointments riling the Foreign Service lifers who have made careers out of mastering the intricacies of diplomacy and statecraft. To a certain extent, that is inevitable, but we must find a way to give our embassies and ambassadors a more dynamic role. We need to encourage some of our most recognized and respected individuals—if not a Ben Franklin, then the best we can do—to assent to public service and send them to foreign capitals, where they can strike a high profile and try to become as popular and influential as Franklin was in Paris. We need to reward the best of our career Foreign Service professionals with appointments appropriate to their respective levels of experience, skill, and passion. And why not have our ambassadors follow in the recent tradition of Secretary Albright and reach out to the public through the media, both in the countries where they serve and here at home, to get people thinking and talking about our place in the world? You, new President, should set the example by doing that yourself and doing your best to ensure that your ambassadors, taken as a whole, could represent the most talented and committed, the most diverse and accomplished, group of U.S. ambassadors ever. The rewards potentially to be gained through such an approach could be incalculable.

9. LESS PARTISAN WARFARE, MORE REAL DEBATE

ormer Senator Howard Baker of Tennessee, an honorable man much liked in both parties, approached me on the floor of the Senate in January 1981 soon after he became Senate Majority Leader for the first time. Baker had been minority leader before that, while I was majority leader, but now we were switching places, and as a man with a long and passionate commitment to making bipartisanship work, he had an offer for me that first day.

"Bob," he said. "I will never know the precedent and rules of the Senate the way you do. You are truly a man of the Senate, steeped in the tradition of the Senate and the knowledge of its procedures. But I'll make you a deal."

We were on the Senate floor and I was listening respectfully, but watched Senator Baker closely to see what he would say next.

"I'll never surprise you if you won't surprise me," he told me.

I met his eye as he made the offer.

"Let me think about it," I told him.

People laugh when Senator Baker tells that story now. They understand that I could have pulled plenty of surprises, given my attention over the years to the details of how the Senate works. But I *did* want to think about it. So I went about my business and gave it some thought and talked to my wife, Erma, about the offer. The next day, I approached the minority leader on the floor.

"All right," I told him.

I always felt that the country benefitted more from bipartisan cooperation than from the endless wrangling for partisan advantage. This strong commitment on my part, dating from my first years in Washington more than half a century ago, does not spring first of all from idealism or civility; no, those are important guiding principles, but even more important is the directive that we are elected by the people to serve, and we can only serve effectively if we look beyond the back-and-forth of partisan confrontation and focus instead on doing the work of the people. It is often noted that nowhere in the Constitution are political parties mentioned, but the Framers were very much aware of the potential of political parties to generate enmity and hamper effective governance.

"Ambition, avarice, personal animosity, party opposition, and many other motives not more laudable than these, are apt to operate as well upon those who support as those who oppose the right side of a question," Thomas Jefferson observed in "Federalist No. 1." "Were there not even these inducements to moderation, nothing could be more ill-judged than that intolerant spirit which has, at all times, characterized political parties. For in politics, as in religion, it is equally absurd to aim at making proselytes by fire and sword. Heresies in either can rarely be cured by persecution."

Once again, I must bow my head and show my respect for Jefferson's foresight. The Founders believed in reason and dignity, not in bending the will of others through the power of "fire and sword." We must bear their wisdom in mind as we strive to do better, bucking up our will with the conviction that it will always be much more effective if we can limit the extent to which partisanship suffuses our work in the Senate and the work of all the people's public servants in Washington.

As the national security adviser to Jimmy Carter, a Democratic President, Zbigniew Brzezinski could not have avoided some partisan leanings, but he has long counseled a higher purpose. And since he has two sons—one a Republican, one a Democrat—he has learned his own lessons about bipartisanship. Dr. Brzezinski gave a much-talked-about speech in Washington in 2003, the wisdom of which more than holds up, I believe.

> I think in the heat of debate Democrats should not be naysayers only, criticizing [he said before the New American Strategies for Security and Peace conference that October]. They certainly should not be cheerleaders as some were roughly a year ago. But they should stress a return to fundamentals in so far as American foreign policy is concerned. Above all else in stressing these fundamentals, Democrats

particularly should insist that the foreign policy of a pluralistic democracy like the United States should be based on bipartisanship because bipartisanship is the means and the framework for formulating policies based on moderation and on the recognition of the complexity of the human condition.

That has been the tradition since the days of Truman and Vandenberg all the way until recent times. That has been the basis for American foreign policy that has been remarkably successful and has led us not only to a triumph in the Cold War but to emerging as the only global superpower with special responsibilities.

Bipartisanship helps to avoid extremes and imbalances. It causes compromises and accommodations. So let's cooperate. Let's cooperate and challenge the administration to cooperate with us because within the administration there are also moderates and people who are not fully comfortable with the tendencies that have prevailed in recent times.

The cynics often try to insist that partisanship has always been just as rampant as it has been in recent years and always will be, but the facts simply do not support that view, as I know from my own experiences over five decades. It is worth remembering, as I am sure you do, that President Clinton, in his early days in office, was encouraged not to rehire a middle-level White House employee named Linda Tripp, given the fact she was a well-known Republican with openly partisan leanings. The President, to his credit, answered that he demanded competence and ability from the people who worked for him in the White House, not a partisan litmus test. Clinton also chose a Republican, former Senator William Cohen, to serve as his secretary of defense. Try to imagine George W. Bush having selected a Democrat to head the Pentagon!

I could spend many pages detailing the extent to which partisanship has plagued Washington in recent years. I could recall the cycle of outrage committed by one side and counteroutrage perpetrated by the other. I could focus in on the Republican effort, led by Karl Rove, to create a so-called permanent Republican majority by baldly enforcing political loyalty in ways that even a bare-knuckled political fighter like Lyndon Johnson would have found over the top—for example, the apparently systematic effort to hire only Republican loyalists in all branches of government, most especially the Justice Department, under the nominal leadership, if that is the word, of the President's friend and fixer Alberto Gonzales.

I prefer, however, to urge that we take it as a given that both sides have become far too committed to partisan warfare and I beg of you, new President, to start at the top with a new emphasis on cooperation and working together. A good way to begin that effort will be to look not at recent history, but at the present and especially the future. This is no time for more political payback. If the previous administration had not left us in so deep a crisis, it might be different, but there simply is no time to waste on that now.

I must revert here to a theme which I have raised perhaps too often in this book, and that is faith. Now that we have spent some time together, in this letter, I know that you are well aware of how important my faith is to me. You know I believe that if we look to the Good Book, if we read the words and heed the message, we can find a way to push past the rancor of the moment and appeal to the best in all of us. We need to forgive and forget and move on. Heed the word of Jesus that one should forgive seventy times seven.

It will not be easy to begin to move beyond chronic partisanship, or at least make enough progress in that direction to create a space in which issues of state can be handled with some measure of seriousness and commitment. Paradoxically, such a move will most likely make one a target of criticism, because influential journalists and others enjoy the status quo, which provides more lively story lines than does bland bipartisan problem-solving. But the turbulence of the moment cannot be allowed to distract one from the larger goal. Progress will take time. You will only truly succeed in this difficult task if a long line of successors continues to build on the beginning you forge of encouraging and protecting a front and central role for bipartisanship cooperation. That is obviously a tall order, but to aim any lower would be to accept that we Americans cannot drive ourselves out of the ditch in which we have been stuck for many years. I refuse to give in to that doubt. I insist on believing in our future and, yes, in you.

I carefully weighed the decision before I decided to confirm my former Senate colleague John Ashcroft as attorney general of the United States. His confirmation hearings were controversial, and to many he came across as the sort of Republican true believer who would put loyalty before the Constitution. I had served with Senator Ashcroft and thought I knew him better than that. I thought he was a man whose basic commitment to the foundations of our democracy was not in question.

"Although I do not agree with all of his views, as I've already indicated, I have no cause to doubt Senator Ashcroft's word or his concern regarding his fealty to an oath that he took before God and man," I said during his Senate confirmation hearing on January 31, 2001. "And as far as I'm personally concerned, it would be an act of supreme arrogance on my part to doubt his intentions to honor that oath. Given Senator Ashcroft's background and positions of which he has been nominated, and his assurances to the Senate that he will faithfully uphold the law of the United States, I shall vote to confirm him."

Speaking to Larry King on CNN, I added, "I'm a legislator. I can have different opinions, but if I were thrust in the position of being Attorney General and I took that oath, I could forget my opinions. God gave man a will. That's what Milton was writing about in *Paradise Lost*. He has the will to put his opinions aside and to uphold his oath to enforce that law."

President Bush's press secretary, Ari Fleischer, cited my position on the nomination in his own remarks to CNN.

"You know, one of the things that the President-elect ran on and he said he would do is acts of bipartisanship, noting people who engage in helping to change the tone in Washington. And I would like to bring to your attention the words of Senator

Robert Byrd, the dean of the Democrats in the Senate . . . and we are very grateful to Senator Byrd for those kind words of bipartisanship and very pleased to see the progress being made with all the nominations on Capitol Hill."

The talk of President Bush working to encourage bipartisanship did not last long, but Attorney General Ashcroft did prove to be a hero of the Bush years. He was a seriously ill man on March 10, 2004, reposing in the intensive-care unit at George Washington University Hospital, when he received an extraordinary visit from Alberto Gonzales, then White House counsel, and Andrew Card, the chief of staff. Given the grave state of Ashcroft's health as he battled a severe case of gallstone pancreatitis, he had named his deputy, James Comey, acting attorney general. In a scene so dramatic it will one day make a gripping scene in a movie, Comey discovered Gonzales and Card were on their way to see Ashcroft to try to compel him to reauthorize the administration's highly questionable domestic surveillance program. Comey hurried over and arrived just before the visitors from the White House did.

"I was angry," Comey later testified before Congress. "I thought I just witnessed an effort to take advantage of a very sick man, who did not have the powers of the Attorney General because they had been transferred to me."

Ashcroft, even in his weakened state, was not about to be steamrolled. As I had said to Larry King: God gave man a will. Ashcroft stood strong for the Constitution, even as Gonzales and Card put extraordinary pressure on him.

"He lifted his head off the pillow and in very strong terms expressed his view of the matter, rich in both substance and fact, which stunned me," Comey testified.

" 'But that doesn't matter,' " Ashcroft said, pointing to Comey, " 'because I'm not the Attorney General. *There* is the Attorney General!' "

One does not have to become a pussycat in order to be an active adherent to bipartisanship. Far from it. One can be at least as much of a fighter as any mere partisan. One must even insist on one's right to sound off now and then, if it is more than called for. In September 2007 I was afforded the great honor of having my portrait hung in the Old Senate Chamber, and I was particularly pleased that the handsome portrait by Tennessee artist Michael Shane Neal showed me with the three pillars of my life—a Bible, my beloved Erma, and the United States Constitution. I was also deeply gratified to note that during the ceremony, the short speeches seemed to be as lively and animated whether they were given by one of my fellow Democrats, such as Ted Kennedy and Tom Daschle, or by Republican friends, such as Howard Baker and John Warner. Given Senator Baker's reputation as a man of humble sincerity, his kind words were deeply gratifying to me.

"I pay tribute to you in many ways but no way greater than the importance of your ability to understand other people's points of view," Senator Baker said. "You've set an example for me and I believe members of the Senate to follow."

Senator Warner, a World War II veteran and former secretary

of the navy, told the gathering a story about a delegation of eight Senators to which we were both attached that traveled to Moscow to meet with Mikhail Gorbachev in September 1985 soon after he became General Secretary of the Soviet Union. As leader of the delegation, I was carrying a letter from President Reagan to Mr. Gorbachev to help pave the way for a constructive meeting between the President and the General Secretary two months later in Geneva, Switzerland.

Some were skeptical when we emerged after our three-and-a-half-hour meeting with Mr. Gorbachev, and I told the press that I found the new Soviet leader "articulate, tough, able, serious," and added that he had twice mentioned the possibility of his introducing "radical proposals" on arms control. We all know now that Mr. Gorbachev's radical proposals—and his call for *glasnost* and *perestroika*—led to one of the most dramatic upheavals of our times and the end of both the Soviet Union and the Cold War.

Senator Warner, speaking at my portrait unveiling, recalled how after the long flight from Washington we had stayed up well into the night working on a short, crisp fifteen-minute statement for me to read. We arrived at the meeting and as the head of the delegation, along with Republican Senator Strom Thurmond, I was the first to shake hands with Mr. Gorbachev.

"[Senator] Thurmond shook Gorbachev's hand," Senator Warner said, "and started to launch into a conversation and the conversation was: 'I know, Mr. Gorbachev, that your father was on the German side in D-Day and I was on the other side. I know your father was wounded, but I'm here to tell you today that I did not fire the shot. . . .'

"Byrd had a very concerned face and said: 'That war is over. You're not going to start another one.' "

Tact is often called for in reconciling the demands of diplomacy and bipartisanship. The story also offers a reminder of how it used to be, and how it must be again: I hand-delivered Reagan's letter to Gorbachev and made clear that I was there with the goal of working hand in hand with the President, rather than at cross-purposes, even though he was very much a Republican and I was very much a Democrat. I credited Gorbachev with being smart and well prepared, but I bristled at the notion that he would put our President at a disadvantage.

"He really isn't ten feet tall," I told the press after our meeting. "He's a younger man, educated, clever and trained as a lawyer and skilled. But you can go down to Sophia or Sutton, West Virginia, and find any number of lawyers who are equally skilled. I have no concern that when it comes to charm and public relations Ronald Reagan can hold his own. We've all seen him do that."

Times have changed since then. It would have been very hard to imagine your immediate predecessor trusting a Democrat with a crucial diplomatic mission like that. The previous administration seemed to think that it had been given all power. We are weaker as a country if the President cannot work with leaders of Congress, as we saw time and time again over the last eight years. For many years in Washington, I would give a talk to the freshman class of every Congress that would come in to start a new term, and I would always emphasize bipartisanship. I would stress that our first responsibility as members of Congress must always be to hold up our institutional role, because that is what checks the executive branch. That's where power really is. It's about time we go back to that again.

10. DON'T FORGET THE BASICS: HAVE THE PATIENCE TO REFLECT

I am aware that in looking back on the humble experiences of growing up in West Virginia coal country, I risk looking like I am trying to paint a Norman Rockwell portrait, but I would submit that when something stays with you throughout your life, there is probably a good reason. As a boy I was always looking for ways to earn a nickel so I could buy myself a toy, usually after weeks of waiting and hoping. Or sometimes I was lucky and a touch of good, old-fashioned industriousness was enough to bring home that elusive goal.

When I was a boy the *Ladies' Home Journal* set up incentives for young boys with energy and persistence to sell subscriptions to their magazine. If you sold enough, you could mail away for something truly wondrous, like a paper balloon. On the bottom of the balloon was a circular attachment etched with a cross, and right there in the crosshairs of that, you placed a candle, and when you lighted it, the paper balloon soon filled with hot air and—this was magical to me—lifted up into the air. I can see it in my mind's eye right now, floating over Stotesbury, a paper balloon rising in the soft wind, barely moving at first and then slowly drifting away. Those are the things that thrilled my heart in those days.

When I was about eight years old I had my eye on a small wooden plane one could order by selling subscriptions. I talked to so many people, trying to sell subscriptions, the humble citizens of our hardworking little community could only marvel at that young Robert Byrd and how he was going to amount to something one day. I didn't know about that: I just wanted my wooden airplane. When it finally arrived, I took it out and was having the time of my life throwing it as high as I could and watching it slice through the air. This was the mid-1920s, not so long after Orville and Wilbur Wright flew a plane in Kitty Hawk, North Carolina, for the first time in 1903, and I had visions of the Wright Brothers dancing in my head as I ran after that small wooden plane to give it another toss. What I did not have visions of was smashing the plane through the window of our neighbor's house, but that was exactly what happened.

I begged the neighbor, Mr. Arch Smith, not to tell my father—or the man I thought of as my father—because I did not want to get a good whipping over this. I knew it would hurt my father to have to do that to me, and it would hurt me, too!

"Please don't tell him," I kept saying. "I'll pay you. I'll run errands for neighbors and pay you."

He accepted that arrangement. It took me seven trips to the store, running errands for different neighbors, to earn the 35 cents to repay Mr. Arch Smith, but he kept his promise and my dad never found out until after I had repaid my debt. I managed to escape a whipping, but I am even more thankful to Mr. Smith for teaching me at a very young age about the need to pay a penalty for misdeeds.

As I think about it now, the episode with Mr. Arch Smith taught me another lesson as well. I did not just run those errands in a few minutes. It took time to find the opportunity, and I had to go to bed at night thinking about what I had done and the consequences of my actions. I slept on it, night after night, and the moral lesson reached me on a deep level. That is why it remains so vivid today.

My mom was not a woman of many words. She always said that a self-braggart is a half-scoundrel. She was a woman of strong faith, hardworking and steady, and believed in action over words. But sometimes at night in our cabin, as she was serving us fresh corn bread, she would see me mulling over this or that and offer me a word of advice.

"Sleep on it, Robert," she would say.

That was just what I did, and I found out that often I had a whole new perspective in the morning. Sometimes it took sleeping on it more than one night. It turns out there is a scientific basis for what she was telling me. As *Nature* magazine reported in January 2004, citing research conducted on a sample of subjects given a full eight-hour sleep and another sample kept awake: " 'Sleep on it' is standard advice to anyone agonizing over a tricky puzzle. A study of mathematical problem-solving has now shown that a good night's rest really does give you a fresh perspective."

When I was in high school we read *Around the World in Eighty Days*. Now we go around the world in eighty minutes. A great emphasis is placed on speed and haste, so as not to allow work to pile up, but I fear that we do not think enough about what is lost in sacrificing the time and quiet of mind necessary to truly deliberate over a question and arrive at a fresh perspective. We cannot even listen, because we do not give ourselves time to hear what a person is trying to tell us. A steady stream of words that gives no one a moment to catch up should never be seen as anything but loud noise. As Mark Twain said, "The right word may be effective, but no word was ever as effective as a rightly timed pause." The art of conversation is in steep decline, because the art of thoughtful consideration has been crowded out of our consciousness. The only way to combat this trend is to insist on time to think and always to be making an effort to improve the mind.

I earned a few raised eyebrows when I started taking law classes as a sitting congressman and kept at it after I moved to the United States Senate in 1959. Fourteen years later, I had a law degree from American University, presented to me personally by our commencement speaker, President John F. Kennedy, who joked in his opening remarks that June 1963 day that "my old Senate colleague Bob Byrd ... has earned his degree through many years of attending night law school while I am earning my [honorary law] degree in the next thirty minutes."

I had no future in mind as a litigator. My goal in studying the law was strengthening my mind. I wanted to have a firmer grasp of the law of the land and the history of our legal tradition. Years later, Richard M. Nixon apparently gave serious consideration to nominating me to become a Supreme Court justice. I passed word that if so great an honor were to be bestowed upon me, I would nevertheless be inclined to demur in favor of continuing my work in the Senate. However, I had to think about it, and I would have never had that opportunity if not for those years of reading law books all weekend long.

Take time in office to reflect, new President. Try to discern if you are following your vision for the future or if you are just casting about from crisis to crisis. Years ago in the Senate I lamented the lack of attention that senators were able to give to the serious business of legislating because of fund-raising needs, serving on too many committees, and generally hectic schedules. I called it fractured attention. In the White House this pace is multiplied times ten. Don't say yes to every plea for just one more fund-raising event or just one more meeting. Budget the time to make sense of it all and to be sure you are steering the ship of state as you intended.

One has to guard against the acceleration of everything in our culture, including thought itself. America has become a place obsessed with speed. We rush to eat, we rush to work, we rush to sleep, we rush to get from one place to another. No one wants to hear an old man complaining about being out of step with the latest technologies, but we can and should ask ourselves about the price we pay for this constant acceleration. My idea of reading involves marking my progress through a good book by feeling the pages against my fingertips. It should take some time to read or to engage in meaningful conversation, and in both cases, if we are in a rush, thinking we have all the answers, we will be deaf to a capacity for surprise. Nothing could be more damaging to the soul.

Even our entertainments have become part of the conspiracy of overstimulation and underreflection that characterizes our times. When I was a boy in West Virginia, it was a major event when we could scrape together two nickels to go to the picture show to watch silent movies with the words off to the side. I would sit there in the movie theater and read the words out loud to show the people how to read. I remember the comedies where the man with his fancy hat would get slapped down by some fella and he would fall and then pop right back up. Oh, how we laughed at that. My favorites were westerns with Jack Hoxie and William Desmond and the short films adapted from the comic strip that starred Andy Gump, whose wife's name was Min, and the comic strip usually ended with him saying, "Ole Min! Ole Min!" Man, I just lived from one Sunday to the next to see what happened to their son, Chester Gump, the next week. He had an uncle, Uncle Ben, who was in Africa searching for diamonds, and of course the cannibals were after him and chewing up people. Oh, this was *great stuff*! To me it was my world. I had no other pastime.

Another favorite of mine was the television program *Gunsmoke*, an old-fashioned, exciting adventure, but there was nothing mean about it. Matt Dillon was the law enforcement officer in his little town, and he had a lady, Kitty, who was his sweetheart. Matt Dillon was always the good guy in the end. He would take care of the roughnecks, but only if it really seemed necessary. (The show was built around a tavern setting, so he didn't clean the place out much.) These ruffians would come in from herding cattle, dusty and tired, and would want a drink of the hard stuff in the morning, and sometimes they would get a little wild. Matt let them go, but if one got a little too rough, he would toss him out. We always knew what Matt would do in a certain situation, and why he was drawing a line where he chose to draw it. In that sense the show had a moral center.

If you look at entertainment today, there are great differences. Movies are either loaded up with a lot of violence and sex, a lot of glitz and glitter, or they jerk from scene to scene with ever more speed and ever less continuity. The pace has become so frenetic that no one can ever relax and sit back for a good story that might be worth reflecting on later.

The world of my boyhood was much different. Imagine a world in which one of the most captivating spectacles was for someone to sit on the flagpole for days on end. People from fifty miles around would come to see a man sitting up on a flagpole. They would fetch him sandwiches and a glass of milk, and he would sit up there for maybe two or three days. They also had marathon dances where couples would dance all day and all night and just barely hold each other up. They would just cling to one another and dance until they were just about to fall over.

To live in a world with such entertainments was to be taught patience from an early age, and that is a virtue which has stood me in good stead my entire life. Not so long ago, it would have seemed numbingly obvious even to speak of the virtues of patience. It was as close as we had to a universal virtue. "Genius is nothing but a greater aptitude for patience," said Ben Franklin, who had to have shown some patience out there with his kite on his way to discovering electricity. Albert Einstein agreed. "It's not that I'm so smart, it's just that I stay with problems longer," he said. And Saint Augustine observed, "Patience is the companion of wisdom."

Yet when we scroll back on the darker days of the previous administration, we see not an inability to practice patience, but an actual contempt for its discipline. As but one example, President Bush met with Spanish Prime Minister José María Aznar on February 22, 2003, at his Crawford, Texas, ranch shortly before the Iraq War. The Spanish daily *El País* obtained a transcript of that meeting, which it published in September 2007, casting an alarming light on the administration's decision-making process leading up to the Iraq War.

As Mark Danner reported in *The New York Review of Books*, "Even in discussing Aznar's main concern, the vital need to give the war international legitimacy by securing a second UN resolution justifying the use of force—a resolution that, catastrophically, was never achieved—little pretense is made that an invasion of Iraq is not already a certainty.

" 'If anyone vetoes,' the President tells Aznar, 'we'll go. Saddam Hussein isn't disarming. We have to catch him right now. Until now we've shown an incredible amount of patience. There are two weeks left. In two weeks we'll be militarily ready. . . . We'll be in Baghdad by the end of March.' "

Aznar, eager to support President Bush, pleaded for time.

"This is like Chinese water torture," the President said, according to the *El País* transcript. "We have to put an end to it."

"I agree, but it would be good to be able to count on as many people as possible," said Aznar. "Have a little patience."

"My patience has run out," Bush said. "I won't go beyond mid-March."

"I'm not asking you to have indefinite patience," Aznar said. "Simply that you do everything possible so that everything comes together."

That, of course, never happened. We will have to take it as a national lesson about the danger of failing to reflect and let all options have the time to run their course. This is a lesson that we can and must apply in diverse contexts, not only when it comes to waging war. To quote the poet Rainer Maria Rilke, "Be patient toward all that is unsolved in your heart and try to love the questions themselves. Do not seek the answers, which cannot be given you because you would not be able to live them. And the point is to live everything. Live the questions."

We all need to live the questions, individually and collectively. That was one of the points I made on the floor of the Senate when I lamented the sleepwalkers who could not snap out of it and understand the gravity of the vital question of what to do about the threat posted by Saddam Hussein. The only way to live the questions is to take the time to do that and to create a space in which the views of Congress and the public they represent are very much a part of the equation. The public needs to be challenged to be involved and kept alert about vital developments of the day, so they have time to think and do not come fresh to every international crisis.

You must lead us toward a new consensus on not settling for fake discussion and fake debate. I have talked of my belief in both challenging and trusting the press, and in this sense of opening room for general reflection—on the part of individuals and on the part of the nation—it becomes imperative to demand that the press push for true discussion. The press ought to be reminded of their acquiescence in efforts to make a sham of real debate, never more blatantly than in January 2006 when the Bush administration gathered many of the finest thinkers in this country on foreign affairs, allegedly to offer advice to the President. To call the session a farce would be to insult the integrity of farce. A Panglossian overview of the situation in Iraq was presented to the thirteen former secretaries of state and defense, all lasting no more than forty minutes, then each of the invited guests was given the chance to speak—for about long enough to clear his or her throat. Some of the participants were so disgusted with the dog-and-pony show, they did not even speak, but President Bush actually pretended as if it were some kind of high-minded exercise.

"I'm most grateful for the suggestions that have been given," he said for the cameras afterward. "We take to heart the advice, we appreciate your experience and we appreciate you taking the time out of your day."

Words so empty that they could blow away on their own, brittle and dry as a dead leaf, should be swept away. They should be seen as the noise they are. Only through a combination of thoughtful and serious words, on the one hand, and a respect for the quiet needed for deliberation and dialogue, on the other, are we ever going to get ourselves back on track as a land truly governed by the people. The Chinese philosopher Confucius once offered: "By three methods we may learn wisdom: First, by reflection, which is noblest; Second, by imitation, which is easiest; and Third, by experience, which is the bitterest." Reflection, true and challenging reflection, must come first. Only with the foundation it provides can we learn wisdom through imitation of the Founding Fathers and the lessons and truth they bequeathed us. Only if we have the ability to think deeper, to think more clearly, can we learn wisdom through experience and set about the hard task of gaining from the dark chapters of our nation's history written in these last few years.

So thank you, new President, for taking this journey on paper with me. My humble and profound hope is that it may leave you with, if nothing else, something to think about.

Senator Robert C. Byrd

NOTES

PAGE

7   Text of President Bush's press conference: http://www.
     whitehouse.gov/news/releases/2004/04/20040413-20.html.

8   Robert Draper, *Dead Certain: The Presidency of George W.
     Bush* (New York: Free Press, 2007).

9   Walter Lippmann, *Public Opinion* (New York: Free Press,
     1997).

11   Hendrik Hertzberg, "Comment," *The New Yorker,* October
     14–21, 2002, page 65.

18   Allan Bloom, *The Closing of the American Mind* (New
     York: Simon & Schuster, 1987).

29   Nancy Gibbs and John F. Dickerson, "Inside the Mind of
     George W. Bush," *Time,* Monday, September 6, 2004: http://
     www.time.com/time/printout/0,8816,995011,00.html.

30   "I Am Not Convinced, Fischer Tells Rumsfeld," *The Daily
     Telegraph,* October 2, 2003.

30   Thom Shanker, "Threats and Responses: Germany; Rums-

feld Rebukes the U.N. and NATO on Iraq Approach," *The New York Times*, February 9, 2003.

39   Andrei Cherny, *The Candy Bombers: The Untold Story of the Berlin Airlift and America's Finest Hour* (New York: Putnam Adult, 2008).

43   "The Shaming of America," *The Economist*, September 10, 2005.

70   Robert C. Byrd, *Child of the Appalachian Coalfields* (West Virginia University Press, 2005).

71   Eric Lichtblau and Carl Hulse, "Democrats Seem Ready to Extend Wiretap Powers," *The New York Times*, October 9, 2007.

76   Terry Golway, *Washington's General: Nathanael Greene and the Triumph of the American Revolution* (New York: Owl Books, 2006).

77   Francis Fukuyama, "The End of History and the Last Man," *The National Interest*, Summer 1989.

78   Francis Fukuyama, *Our Posthuman Future: Consequences of the Biotechnology Revolution* (New York: Farrar, Straus and Giroux, 2002).

110   Daniel Okrent, "The Public Editor: Weapons of Mass Destruction? Or Mass Distraction?" *The New York Times*, May 30, 2004.

113   Ann McFeatters, "Thank *You*, Ms. Thomas," *Ms.*, Summer 2006.

119   Thomas L. Friedman, *The World Is Flat: A Brief History of*

the Twenty-first Century (New York: Farrar, Straus and Giroux, 2005).

124 Stanley Milgram, *Obedience to Authority: An Experimental View* (London: Tavistock Publications, 1974).

125 Dana Milbank and Claudia Deane, "Hussein Link to 9/11 Lingers in Many Minds," *The Washington Post*, September 6, 2003.

131 Steve Kettmann, "Bush's Secret Weapon," Salon.com, March 20, 2000.

135 Richard Milhous Nixon, *RN: The Memoirs of Richard Nixon* (New York: Grosset & Dunlap, 1978).

137 Jake Tapper, "Did Bush Bungle Relations with North Korea?" Salon.com, March 15, 2001.

143 Henry Ford, *My Life and Work* (New York: Cosimo Classics, 2007).

144 Samantha Power, *A Problem from Hell: America and the Age of Genocide* (New York: Basic Books, 2002).

147 Stacy Schiff, *A Great Improvisation: Franklin, France, and the Birth of America* (New York: Henry Holt and Company, 2005).

153 Zbigniew Brzezinski, New American Strategies, Address to the New American Strategies Conference, October 28, 2003: http://www.newamericanstrategies.org/articles/display.asp?fldArticleID=68.

170 Mark Danner, "The Moment Has Come to Get Rid of Saddam," *The New York Review of Books*, November 8, 2007.

INDEX

"ABC foreign policy" (Anything But Clinton), 136
ABC News, 111, 112
accountability, President's need for, 97–108
  Harry Truman's "The Buck Stops Here" model of accountability, 99–100
  Iran-contra scandal, cover-up in, 102–7
Acton, Lord (John Dalberg), 11
Adams, Abigail, 2
Adams, John, 2
Aeroflot, 81
Ahmadinejad, Mahmoud, 3, 133
Air Force Two, 81
Albright, Madeleine, 128–29, 150
  on media campaigns, 128–29
al Qaeda, 125
ambassadors, U.S., 146–50
  Foreign Service professionals, 149
  Fox, Sam, 147, 148
  Franklin, Benjamin, 147–48
  political appointments, 149
  President as Ambassador Supreme, 142
American History, An (Muzzey), 57
American people
  accepting an honest "no" as an answer from elected officials, 89–90
  becoming familiar with history, 75–86

Iraq War, mind-set regarding, 124–26
  opinion that the country is on the wrong track, 59
  participating in government at every level, need for, 86
  polling about the Constitution, 70
  voting, need for, 86
Anna Lindh Professor of Practice of Global Leadership and Public Policy, 144
Argentina, 140
Aristotle, 35
Around the World in Eighty Days, 166
Ashcroft, John, 156–59
  Byrd's support of, as U.S. attorney general, 156–58
  illness of, 158–59
Auschwitz, 47, 48
"Axis of Evil", 137
Aznar, José María, meeting with President Bush about administration's decision about Iraq War, 170–71

Baker, Howard, 151–52, 159
Baker, James, 95
Battle of the Bulge, 39
Bay of Pigs invasion, 5–6, 41
BBC. *See* British Broadcasting Corporation

Berlin, 40, 47, 78, 99. *See also* Germany
  Berlin Airlift, 40, 99
  Berlin Wall, 48, 78
  Jewish community of, 47
Bertrand de Jouvenel, 35
Bible passages
  Ecclesiastes, 50, 79
  Job 1:21, 2
  John 8:31, 96
  Luke 5:12, 44
  Philippians 2:3–8, 8–9
Bill of Rights, 70. *See also* Constitution, U.S.
bin Laden, Osama, 55
bipartisan cooperation between political
    parties
  need for, 151–62
  President Bill Clinton and, 154–55
  Zbigniew Brzezinski about, 153–54
Blair, Tony, 140
Bloom, Allan, 18–20
  on faith and moral education, 19
  upbringing of, 19–20
Boland Amendment, 102
Bolshevik Revolution, 110
Bonds, Barry, 25
Brady, Nicholas F., 105
Brezhnev, Leonid, 23, 81–82, 134
  Senate Majority Leader Byrd's 1979 visit
    with, 81–82, 134
Brinkley, David, 109
British Broadcasting Corporation (BBC),
    43–44
Brown, Michael, 42
Bryant, William Cullen, 88–89
Brzezinski, Zbigniew, 152–53
"The Buck Stops Here" as Harry Truman's
    model of accountability, 99–100
Bullock, Alan, 83
Burke, Edmund, 12
Bush, Barbara, 42–43

Bush, George H.W.
  Condoleezza Rice in administration of,
    130, 131
  Iran-contra scandal, 104–7
  pardons of Caspar Weinberger and
    others involved in Iran-contra
    scandal, 106
  as vice president to Ronald Reagan,
    104–5
Bush, George W., 6–13, 25, 28, 29, 38, 42,
    69, 79, 87, 124, 132, 142, 154, 157,
    170–71
  "ABC foreign policy" (Anything But
    Clinton), 136
  administration's continual lies, 93–95
  administration's domestic surveillance
    program, 158
  administration's January 2006 session on
    foreign affairs, 172–73
  administration's fearmongering after
    September 11, 2001, 30–31, 55. *See
    also* Hussein, Saddam
  administration's policies toward North
    Korea, 136–38
  administration's relation with Turkey,
    141
  administration's role in influencing
    worldwide anti-Americanism, 146
  family history, 94
  failings of, 25
  Garry Kasparov's criticism of adminis-
    tration, 132–33
  Hurricane Katrina and, 42–44
  inability to admit mistakes, 6–8
  interviews, 8, 29, 95, 172–73
  media, dealings with, 112–16. *See also*
    interview; press conferences
  "National Security Strategy of the
    United States of America" Septem-
    ber 2002, 10

Patriot Act, 71
press conferences, 6–7, 42, 112–14
religion and, 8, 11, 13
speech in August 2007 about Iraq War
 and Vietnam War, 38
speech in October 2007 about U.S. economy, 61
undermining the Constitution, 10
Bush, Prescott, 93
Bush 43 administration. *See* Bush, George W.
Byrd, Erma (author's wife), 65, 152, 159
Byrd, Marjorie (author's daughter), 97
Byrd, Mona (author's daughter), 97
Byrd, Robert C.
 address at West Virginia University, 70
 advice to new President
  accountability, building presidency
   around, 97–108
  bipartisanship, establish within Washington, 151–62
  Constitution, adhering to and teaching people about, 65–73
  diplomacy, establishing with other
   countries, 123–34, 135–50
  fireside chats, establishing dialogue
   with citizens by having, 53–63
  history, importance of understanding,
   14, 22, 38, 48, 75–86
  press, the, working with, even if it's
   uncomfortable, 109–21
  reflection, making the time for regu-
   lar, 163–73
  truth, telling the, 87–96
 Clinton impeachment and, 91–93
 dealings with the press as Senate Majority Leader, 117–18
 during John Ashcroft Senate confirmation, 157–58
 early years of, 4, 39, 45, 79, 88, 163–69
 on House Foreign Affair Committee, 141

love of music, 49
love of reading, 45–46, 168
Nevada trip to possibly witness a nuclear
 explosion, 80
parents' influence, 4, 165
portrait hanging in Old Senate Chamber, 159
Senate floor remarks
 about Iraq War, 31–33
 about Saddam Hussein, 171–72
 about Republican scheme to bypass
  the rules of, 83–84, 85
 about North Korea, 138
Soviet Union trip as Senate Majority
 Leader (1979), 23, 81–82, 134
Turkey trip (1955), 141
Byron, Lord (George Gordon), 79

Caesar, Julius, 75
California, 36–37
Canada, 140
*Candy Bombers, The: The Untold Story of
 the Berlin Airlift and America's
 Finest Hour* (Cherny), 39
Canfil, Fred, 99
Card, Andrew, 158–59
Carter, Jimmy, 12, 23, 152
Castro, Fidel, 5–6
Cato the Elder, 45
Central Intelligence Agency (CIA), 102
change, concept of, 36, 77, 128
 addiction of a nation to, 77
 as cyclical, 128
 surprising consequences of change, 36
Charleston Municipal Auditorium, 97
Chavez, Hugo, 3
checks and balances in U.S. government,
 10, 12, 13
Cheney, Dick, 104, 124, 132, 137
 as assistant minority leader, 104

Cheney, Dick (*continued*)
Iraq War and, 124, 132
North Korea, attitude toward, 137
Cherny, Andrei, 39–41
about Berlin Airlift, in *The Candy
Bombers*, 40–41
CIA. *See* Central Intelligence Agency
Civilian Conservation Corps, 37
Clark, Wesley, 125
Clinton, Bill, 90–93, 106, 113, 128, 136–39,
142–43, 154–55
administration's foreign policies,
136–39, 142–43
administration's policies toward North
Korea, 136–39
bipartisanship of, 154–55
economy under administration's tenure,
90, 142
Helen Thomas and, 113
impeachment trial in Senate, 91–92
pardon of Marc Rich, 106
Closing of the American Mind, The
(Bloom), 18–20
CNN, 157
Cohen, William, 154
Cold War, 11, 24, 78–80, 160
Gorbachev's influence on end of, 160
Reagan's claims of U.S. weakness against
the Soviets, 24
U.S. place in the world after the end of
the Cold War, 78–80
Comey, James, 158–59
Confucius, 173
Congress, U.S. *See also* bipartisan
cooperation between political parties
Byrd's Senate floor speech about Repub-
lican scheme to bypass the rules of,
83–84, 85
Byrd's speech during John Ashcroft Sen-
ate confirmation, 157–58

as institution to avoid misuse of executive power, 16
need to work with President in a bipartisan fashion, 27, 151–62
President Clinton's impeachment trial,
91–92
role in Iraq War, 28, 70–71
Senate oratory as lost art, 85
Conquest of Gaul, The (Caesar), 75
Constitution, U.S., 2, 13, 22, 25, 49, 54, 58,
59, 65–73, 102, 143, 152
as drafted by Founding Fathers, 67–69
having faith in, 22
Iran-contra scandal, as direct flouting of,
102
poll numbers that show public's lack of
knowledge about, 70
President George W. Bush's undermining
of, 102–4
President Franklin Roosevelt's remarks
about, 58
role of the new President to teach people
about, 65–73
threatening of, 49, 54, 59, 143
Continental army, 76
Continental Congress, 147
Cornwallis, Lord Charles, 76
Cuba, 5–6

Daily Breeze, 113
Danner, Mark, 170–71
Darfur, 145
Darwin, Charles, 18
Daschle, Tom, 159
Dead Certain (Draper), 8
Death March, 47
Declaration of Independence, 147
Defense Department, Boland Amendment
and, 102
Defoe, Daniel, 45

democracy
    flaws in, 15–16, 35
    need for public officials to tell the truth, 87
    power of, 120–21
    the role of the press and, 109–21
    Walter Lippmann's observation about,
        15–16
Desmond, William, 168
dialogue by elected officials
    with constituents, 49, 61–62, 146
    FDR's fireside chats, 59–61
Dickerson, John F., 29
Dillon, Matt, 168
diplomacy, overseas, 27–28, 34, 123–34,
        135–50
    ambassadors in other countries, having
        better, 146–50
    influencing rest of the world not only by
        military power, 135–50
    "photo-op" diplomacy, doing better
        than, 123–34
    understanding the art and value of, 142
    U.S. reacquiring credibility, 34, 140–41,
        143–44
Dole, Bob, 104
Donaldson, Sam, 111, 112
Draper, Robert, 8

Ecclesiastes, 50, 79
Economist magazine, 43
economy, U.S.
    President George W. Bush's speech in
        October 2007, 61
    under President Clinton's tenure, 90, 142
Edison, Thomas, 145
Eichmann, Adolf, 123
Einstein, Albert, 18, 170
Eisenhower, Dwight, 5
El País, 170–71
Emerson, Ralph Waldo, 9, 18, 126

Enabling Law, the, 84
"End of History and the Last Man, The"
        (Fukuyama), 77–78
Etruscans, 45
European Union, Turkey and, 27–28

faith
    importance of, 2–5, 12–13, 17, 20–22
    moral education and, 19
Federal Emergency Management Academy
        (FEMA), 42
federal government, three branches of, 70
Federalist Papers, The, 11, 69, 86, 101, 107,
        152
    "Federalist No. 1", 152
    "Federalist No. 49", 101
    "Federalist No. 51", 11
    "Federalist No. 70", 107
FEMA. *See* Federal Emergency Manage-
        ment Academy
fireside chat, 53–63
Fischer, Joschka, 30, 32
Fleischer, Ari, 157
Ford, Gerald, 2, 4
Ford, Henry, 143
Foreign Service, 149
Forrestal, James, 41
Fort McHenry, 66
Founding Fathers, 10, 13, 16–17, 22, 45, 67,
        68, 84, 107, 110, 148
    about accountability, 107
    about checks and balances in govern-
        ment, 10
    drafting the Constitution, 68
    rule of law, importance of, 84
    tug-of-war between press and, 110
Fox, Sam, 148
France, as U.S. ally, 29, 33
Franklin, Benjamin, 147–48, 149, 170
    about patience, 170

Franklin, Benjamin (*continued*)
  accomplishments, 147
  as U.S. ambassador to France, 148, 149
Frederick the Great of Prussia, 75
Friedman, Thomas L., 119–20
Fukuyama, Francis, 77–78
fund-raising versus connecting with
    people, 146

Gann, Paul, 36
Germany, 29, 30, 33, 39–40, 46–48, 99,
    140
  Berlin Airlift, 40, 99
  Berlin Wall, 48, 78
  Dresden, firebombing of, 86
  objection to Iraq War, 30, 32, 48
  Third Reich, 46, 124
  as U.S. ally, 29, 30, 48
  in World War II, 39, 46–48
Gingrich, Newt, 90
Golway, Terry, 76
Gonzales, Alberto, 154, 158–59
  visit to John Ashcroft to compel him to
      reauthorize the Bush administra-
      tion's domestic surveillance pro-
      gram, 158
Gorbachev, Mikhail, 38, 131, 160–61
  President George H.W. Bush's intro-
      duction of Condoleezza Rice to,
      131
  senatorial meeting with (September
      1985), 160–61
  summit with President Ronald Reagan
      in Reykjavik, Iceland (1986), 38
Gore, Al, 142
Gramm, Phil, 85
Great Britain, 43, 140
Great Depression, 37–38, 50, 54
  Franklin Roosevelt's social programs
      during, 37–38

*Great Improvisation, A: Franklin, France,
    and the Birth of America* (Shiff),
    147–48
Greene, Nathanael, 75–77
  as an example of the "new American
      idea", 76
Greensboro, North Carolina, 75
Gulf War, 31
Gump, Andy, 168
Gump, Ben, 168
Gump, Chester, 168
Gump, Min, 168
Gunsmoke, 168–69

Halvorsen, Gail, 40
Hamilton, Alexander, 12, 107
  about the plurality of the Executive
      branch, in "Federalist No. 70", 107
Hamlet, 10
Hegel, Georg Wilhelm Friedrich, 78
Hertzberg, Hendrik, 11–12
higher education, faith and, as written by
    Allan Bloom, 19–20
Hiroshima, Japan, atomic bombing of, 80,
    99
history, importance of understanding, 14,
    22, 38, 48, 75–86
  Nathanael Green's influence during the
      Revolutionary War, 75–77
  Cold War, end of the, 77–78
  human nature not changing despite his-
      toric events, 79
  understanding the evil of Hitler and
      Stalin, 82–83
Hitler, Adolf, 47, 82–84, 85, 93
  quote about lying, 93
  Senator Byrd's mention of Hitler on Sen-
      ate floor when talking about Re-
      publican scheme to bypass the rules
      of Congress, 83–84

House Foreign Affair Committee, 141

Hoxie, Jack, 168

human nature not changing despite historic events, 79

Hurricane Katrina, 9, 41–44, 144
Barbara Bush's remarks about Katrina
refugees, 42–43
BBC look at, 44
President George W. Bush's actions and
words after, 42

Hurt, John, 95

Hussein, Saddam, 110, 124–125, 126,
170–71
American people's belief about Saddam
Hussein's involvement with Sep-
tember 11 attacks, 124–25
President George W. Bush to José María
Aznar about, 170–71

inaugural speeches by Presidents
John F. Kennedy (January 20, 1961), 62
Franklin Delano Roosevelt (March 4,
1933), 53, 56–57, 58

influence, U.S. role in world, 34, 135–50
having better ambassadors in other
countries, 146–50
influencing rest of the world not only by
military power, 135–50
need for U.S. to reacquire credibility
around the world, 34, 140–41,
143–44

Instructions to His Generals (Frederick the
Great), 75

International Security Conference (39th
Annual), 30

interviews by President George W. Bush,
29, 95, 172–73

Iran, 3

Iran-contra scandal, 102–7
George H.W. Bush's role, 104–7

Ronald Reagan and his adminstration's
roles in, 103–5

Iraq, 27. *See also* Iraq War

Iraq Study Group, 95

Iraq War, 9, 28, 33, 38, 48, 95, 110,
114–20, 124, 130, 132, 144–45,
170–71
Colin Powell and, 130
Congress's role in, 28, 30–33
Garry Kasparov's attitude about, 132
Iraq Study Group, 95
Joschka Fischer's stance on, 30, 32
José María Aznar's stance on, 170–71
media and, 110, 114–20
Milgram experiments, as explanation of
public's reaction to, 123–24
President George W. Bush's constant lies
about, 95
President George W. Bush's comments
about, 170–71
Robert Byrd's speech on Senate floor,
30–33
Samantha Power about, 144–45

Jarvis, Howard, 36

Jefferson, Thomas, 14, 17, 69, 152–53
"Federalist No. 1", 69
letter describing need for open public
dissent to ensure government honesty, 17

Jesus of Nazareth, 8–9, 44

Jewish community of Berlin, 47–48

Job 1:21, 2

John 8:31, 96

John F. Kennedy School of Government,
144

Johnson, Lyndon, 135, 154

Kasparov, Garry, 132–33

Kennedy, John F., 5–6, 62, 113, 166

Kennedy, John F. (*continued*)
 inaugural speech (January 20, 1961), 62
 the press and, 113
 John F. Kennedy School of Government,
  144
Kennedy, Ted, 159
Kerry, John, 148–49
Key, Francis Scott, 66
Khe Sanh, 41
Khomeini, Ayatollah, 101
Kim Jong I, 136
Kim Jong Il, 137, 138
King, Larry, 157, 158
Kissinger, Henry, 147
Kitty from *Gunsmoke*, 168
Knyphausen, Wilhelm von, 77
Korea, 99
 North Korea, U.S. relations with,
  136–39
Krock, Arthur, 56
Kurdistan, U.S. backing of Iraqi Kurds in,
 141

Ladies' Home Journal, 163
Lenin, Vladimir Illyich, 93
 quote about lying, 93
letters by President Thomas Jefferson, 17
Lewinsky, Monica, 91
Lippmann, Walter, 9, 15–16, 110, 116–17,
 119
 about democracy, 15–16
 on self-important political commentators, 116–17
lies at the top of government, 87–96
 President George W. Bush and his administration, 87, 93
 President Bill Clinton, 91
 President Richard Nixon, 91
Losing America (Byrd), 10
Luke 5:12, 44

Madison, James, 1–2, 11, 12, 101
 in "Federalist No. 51", 11
 first night in White House, 1–2
Maher, Bill, 132
Marine One, 111
Marshall Plan, 99, 145
McCarthy, Joseph, 53
McFeatters, Ann, 113
media, the, 109–21
 Byrd's belief in challenging and trusting,
  109–21, 172
 dealings with President George W. Bush,
  112–16
 dealings with President Reagan, 111–12
 dealings with Senate Majority Leader
  Byrd, 117–18
 Helen Thomas, treatment of, 113–18
 Madeleine Albright and, 129
 President Truman's remarks about the
  need for an active and involved
  press, 117
 tug-of-war between press and elected of-
  ficials, 110
Meese, Edwin, 104
Meet the Press, 126
Merze, Charles, 110
Milgram, Stanley, 123–24
Milton, John, 157
"Ministry of Truth," 71–72
Ms. magazine, 113
Mueller, John, 125
music
 Byrd's love of music, 49
 Estrongo Nachama, during World War
  II, 47–48
 need for, 48–49
Mussolini, Benito, 83
Muzzey, David Saville, 57
My Life and Work (Ford), 143
Myers, Lisa, 92

Nachama, Estrongo, 47–48

Nagasaki, Japan, atomic bombing of, 80, 99

National Interest, The, 78

National Security Agency, 71

National Security Council, 130

"National Security Strategy of the United States of America" September 2002 by Bush administration, 10

National Socialists, 39

NATO. *See* North Atlantic Treaty Organization

Nature magazine, 165

NBC Nightly News, 92

Neal, Michael Shane, 159

New American Strategies for Security and Peace conference, 153

New Orleans. *See* Hurricane Katrina

news conferences. *See* press conferences

New Yorker magazine, 11

New York Review of Books, The, 170–71
  transcript of José María Azar meeting with President Bush about administration's decision about Iraq War, 170–71

New York Times, The, 47–48, 56, 71, 105, 110, 119–20, 148–49
  about Congressmen being afraid of being called soft on terrorism, 71
  about Estrongo Nachama, 47–48
  about Franklin Delano Roosevelt's inaugural speech, 56
  about Iran-contra scandal and Vice President Bush's involvement, 105
  about U.S. involvement in Iraq War, 110
  editorial piece about appointment of Sam Fox as ambassador,
  Thomas Friedman's column about Iraq War, 119–20

Nicaragua, 102

Nietzsche, Friedrich, 87

Nigeria, 140

1984 (Orwell), 71, 95

Nitze, Paul, 41

Nixon, Richard M., 91, 135, 149, 167
  consideration of Robert Byrd for Supreme Court Justice, 167
  early days in White House, 135
  foreign embassy appointments, 149

North Atlantic Treaty Organization (NATO), 27, 99, 125, 141

North Korea, U.S. relations with, 136–39
  Colin Powell's stance on, 136–37
  President Bill Clinton's foreign policy, 136
  President George W. Bush's foreign policy, 136–39

nuclear explosion
  Congressman Byrd's traveling to Nevada to possibly witness a, 80
  Hiroshima and Nagasaki, 80, 99

Obedience to Authority: An Experimental View (Milgram), 124

O'Donnell, Rosie, 25

officials, elected
  need for communication with constituents, 49, 59–62, 126–28, 146
  saying "no", 89–90
  telling the truth, 87–96

Ohio State University, 125

Okrent, Daniel, 110

Orwell, George, 34, 71–72

Our Posthuman Future: Consequences of the Biotechnology Revolution (Fukuyama), 78

overseas diplomacy, 27–28, 34, 123–34, 135–50
  ambassadors in other countries, having better, 146–50
  influencing rest of the world not only by military power, 135–50

overseas diplomacy (*continued*)
"photo-op" diplomacy, doing better
than, 123–34
U.S. reacquiring credibility, 34, 140–41,
143–44
Ovid, 46

Pakistan, 139
Paradise Lost (Milton), 157
pardons by President, 106
Patriot Act, 71
patriotism
devaluation of, 66
Mark Twain definition, 125
Pew Global Attitudes Survey, 139
Philippians 2:3–8, 8–9
Phoenix Chamber of Commerce, Ronald
Reagan's 1961 speech to, 23
photo-op diplomacy, doing better than,
123–34
Madeleine Albright's use of media to ad-
vocate her views and U.S. interests,
129–30
Condoleezza Rice as secretary of state,
130–33
the need for context, 126
Pilgrim, Billy, 86
Plato, 87
Poindexter, John, 104
Poland, 140
Polonius, 10
polling
American people's belief about Saddam
Hussein's involvement with Sep-
tember 11 attacks, 124
American people's knowledge about the
Constitution, 70
American people's feelings about U.S.
being on the wrong track, 59
worldwide view of U.S., 139–40

Popper, Karl, 21
Powell, Colin, 29–30, 130, 136–37
opinions about North Korea, 136–37
speech to UN about Iraq and alleged
weapons of destruction, 29–30,
130
power, obscene misuse of, 83, 84. *See also*
September 11, 2001, aftermath of
Power, Samantha, 144–45
President, role of the, 7
as Ambassador Supreme, 142
conveying optimism, 59–60, 62–63
inviting dialogue, 14–15, 60. *See also*
fireside chats
need for bipartisan cooperation with
Congress, 151–62
representing all citizens, 14, 25–26
telling the truth, 87–96
use of faith, 20–21
use of power, 14, 16
Presidential pardons, 106
Bill Clinton's pardon of Marc Rich, 106
George H. W. Bush's pardons of Caspar
Weinberger and others involved in
Iran-contra scandal, 106
Presidential words. *See also* speeches by
Presidents
interviews by President George W. Bush,
29, 95, 172–73
letters by President Thomas Jefferson, 17
press conferences by Presidents, 5–6,
6–7, 42, 112–14
President Truman's remarks about the
need for an active and involved
press, 117
speeches by Presidents
Bush, George W. about Iraq War and
Vietnam War, 38
Bush, George W., 61
Ford, Gerald, 2

Kennedy, John F., about Bay of Pigs, 6
Kennedy, John F., inaugural speech
    (January 20, 1961), 62
Reagan, Ronald (as governor), 23–24
Roosevelt, Franklin Delano, fireside
    chats, 59–61
Roosevelt, Franklin Delano, first inau-
    gural address (March 4, 1933), 53,
    56–57, 58
Truman, Harry, 3, 97
press, the. *See also* press conferences by
    Presidents
Byrd's belief in challenging and trusting,
    109–21, 172
dealings with President George W. Bush,
    112–16
dealings with President Reagan,
    111–12
dealings with Senate Majority Leader
    Byrd, 117–18
Helen Thomas, treatment of, 113–18
Madeleine Albright and, 129
President Truman's remarks about the
    need for an active and involved
    press, 117
tug-of-war between press and elected of-
    ficials, 110
press conferences by Presidents
Bush, George W., 6–7, 42, 112–14
Eisenhower, Dwight, 5
Kennedy, John F., 5–6
*Problem from Hell, A: America and the Age
    of Genocide* (Power), 144
Proposition 13 (California), 36
Public Opinion (Lippmann), 9, 15–16
Putin, Vladimir, 132–33

Rayburn, Sam, 98
Reagan, Ronald, 22–24, 36–38, 102–4, 107,
    111–12, 149, 160, 161

anti-Communist stance, 23–24
as governor of California, 23, 36–37
Iran-contra scandal, 102–4, 107
the press and, 111–12
Soviet Union and, 23, 38
reflection
Byrd's belief in failure to reflect, 172
taking time for, 163–73
Regan, Donald, 104
reporters, 109–21. *See also* press confer-
    ences
dealings with President George W. Bush,
    112–16
dealings with President Reagan, 111–12
dealings with Senate Majority Leader
    Byrd, 117–18
Madeleine Albright and, 129
President Truman's remarks about, 117
tug-of-war with elected officials, 110
Revolutionary War, 65, 75–77
Nathanael Greene's contributions, 75–77
Reykjavik, Iceland, 38
Rice, Condoleezza, 31, 100, 124, 130–32,
    133
in administration of George W. Bush,
    130–32
interview with Salon.com, 131
public demeanor, 133
as Secretary of State, 31, 124, 133
Rich, Marc, 106
Rilke, Rainer Maria, 171
Roberts, Cokie, 91
Robinson Crusoe (Defoe), 46
Rockwell, Norman, 163
Roman Empire, United States and, 11, 72, 86
Roosevelt, Eleanor, 98
Roosevelt, Franklin Delano, 37–38, 53, 56,
    58, 60–61, 93, 98
about lying, 93
commonsense wisdom, 54

Roosevelt, Franklin Delano (*continued*)
    fireside chat, 59–61
    first inaugural address (March 4, 1933),
        53, 56–57, 58
    social programs during Great Depres-
        sion, 37–38
Rotary Club, 146
Rove, Karl, 154
Rumsfeld, Donald, 29, 30–31
    at 39th Annual International Security
        Conference in Munich, 30
Russia, 139. *See also* Soviet Union

Saint Augustine, 170
Salon.com, Condoleezza Rice interview
    with, 131
SALT II. *See* Strategic Arms Limitation
    Agreement
Santorum, Rick, 85
Schweiker, Richard, 36
Scott, Walter, 87
Secretary of States
    Albright, Madeleine, 128–29, 150
    Kissinger, Henry, 147
    Powell, Colin, 29–30, 130, 136–37
    Rice, Condoleezza, 31, 100, 124, 130–31,
        133
    Shultz, George, 104, 105
Senate Appropriations Committee, 41
September 11, 2001, aftermath of, 10, 55,
    69–70, 72, 120, 124–25
    American people's belief about Saddam
        Hussein's involvement with Sep-
        tember 11 attacks, 124
    Bush extends state of emergency every
        year, 69–70
    fearmongering, 55
    Patriot Act, 71
    unleashing of perpetual fear into the
        lives of Americans, 72

Shakespeare, William, 9–10, 46
    Hamlet, 9–10
Shiff, Stacy, 147–48
Shultz, George, 104, 105
    contention that Vice President Bush was
        involved in Iran-contra scandal,
        105
Skull and Bones, 94
Slaughterhouse Five (Vonnegut), 86
Smith, Arch, 164–65
Smith, William S., 17
Smith, Winston, 72, 95
Society of Professional Journalists, 113
Soviet Union, 23, 38, 81, 99, 131–32
    Senate Majority Leader Byrd's trip to, 23,
        81–82, 134
speeches by Presidents. *See also* press con-
        ference by Presidents
    Bush, George W. about Iraq War and
        Vietnam War, 38
    Bush, George W., 61
    Ford, Gerald, 2
    Kennedy, John F., about Bay of Pigs, 6
    Kennedy, John F., inaugural speech (Jan-
        uary 20, 1961), 62
    Reagan, Ronald (as governor), 23–24
    Roosevelt, Franklin Delano, fireside
        chats, 59–61
    Roosevelt, Franklin Delano, first inaugu-
        ral address (March 4, 1933), 53,
        56–57, 58
    Truman, Harry, 3, 97
Stalin, 82–83, 84
Stanford University, 130
"Star-Spangled Banner, The," 66
Stephanopoulos, George, 95
Stone, Harlan F., 89
Stotesbury, West Virginia, 79
Strategic Arms Limitation Agreement
    (SALT II), 23, 81

Straw, Jack, 133
Swift Boat Veterans for Truth, 148

Third Reich, 46, 93, 124
This Week, 92, 95, 112
  President George W. Bush's remarks
    about strategies of in Iraq War,
    95
  Senator Byrd's remarks on President
    Clinton's impeachment trial, 92
Thomas, Helen, 113–16
Thurmond, Strom, 160
Time magazine, interview with President
    Bush in September 2004, 29
"Today and Tomorrow" column, 116–17
Tolstoy, Leo, 3
Tripp, Linda, 154
Truman, Harry, 1, 2–3, 5, 14, 40, 41,
    97–100, 101–2, 108, 117, 153
  about the need for an active and
    involved press, 117
  "The Buck Stops Here," expression,
    99–100
  decisions and accomplishments as Presi-
    dent, 99
  establishing accountability in adminis-
    tration, 102
  supporting Byrd for U.S. Senate, 97
  swearing in as President, 98
truth, telling the, 87–96
  need for public officials to tell the truth,
    87
  lies by President George W. Bush and his
    administration, 87, 93
  lies by President Bill Clinton, 91
  lies by President Richard Nixon, 91
Turkey, 27, 140–41
  Byrd trip to, 140
  U.S. relations with, 140–41
Twain, Mark, 53, 58, 77, 88, 93, 125, 166

United Kingdom, 43, 140
United Nations, 29–30, 31, 145
  arms inspectors, 31
  Colin Powell's speech about Iraq and al-
    leged weapons of destruction,
    29–30, 130
United Press International (UPI), 113
United States
  American people's knowledge about the
    Constitution, 70
  American people's feelings about U.S.
    being on the wrong track, 59
  Constitution of, 2, 13, 22, 25, 49, 54, 58,
    59, 65–73, 102, 143, 152
  diplomacy with Allies, need for, 33–34
  taking values and principles for granted,
    55, 59
  worldwide opinions of, 139–43

Vandenberg, Hoyt, 153
Venezuela, 3
Vietnam War
  George W. Bush speech in August 2007
    about Iraq War and, 38
  Viet Nam Situation Report, 135
Vonnegut, Kurt, 86

Walsh, Lawrence, 106
Walt, Steve, 145
Warner, John, 159, 160
Washington, George, 13–14, 75, 117
Washington Goes to War (Brinkley), 109
Washington Post, The, 94, 105, 124, 125
*Washington's General: Nathanel Greene and
    the Triumph of the American Revo-
    lution* (Golway), 76
Weinberger, Caspar, 106
West Virginia University, 70
White House News Photographers' Associ-
    ation (1988), 111–12

Wilson, Woodrow, 1
Wolf Creek Hollow (West Virginia), Byrd's
    life in, 4, 35, 65, 88, 133
Wolfowitz, Paul, 18
Works Progress Administration, 37
World Is Flat, The: A Brief History of the
    Twenty-first Century (Friedman),
    119
World News Tonight, 91
World War II, 3, 39, 46–47, 54, 99
    accomplishments of victory in, 39
    lessons learned from, 46–47

President Truman's radio announcement
    of end of, 3
Wright, Jim, 104
Wright, Orville, 164
Wright, Wilbur, 164

Yale University researcher Stanley Milgram
    experiments, 123–24
Yalta, 81
YMCA, 146

Zablocki, Clement, 141